PORTFOLIO
CARAVANS

SCOTT C. LEVI is associate professor of Central Asian History at Ohio State University. His research focuses on the social and economic history of Central Asia in the broader context of the early modern Indo-Islamic world.

GURCHARAN DAS is a world-renowned author, commentator and public intellectual. His bestselling books include *India Unbound*, *The Difficulty of Being Good* and *India Grows at Night*. His other literary works consist of a novel, *A Fine Family*, a book of essays, *The Elephant Paradigm*, and an anthology, *Three Plays*. A graduate of Harvard University, Das was CEO of Procter & Gamble, India, before he took early retirement to become a full-time writer. He lives in Delhi.

THE STORY OF INDIAN BUSINESS
Series Editor: Gurcharan Das

THE STORY OF INDIAN BUSINESS

CARAVANS

*Punjabi Khatri Merchants
on the Silk Road*

SCOTT C. LEVI

Introduction by
Gurcharan Das

PORTFOLIO
PENGUIN

An imprint of Penguin Random House

PORTFOLIO

USA | Canada | UK | Ireland | Australia
New Zealand | India | South Africa | China | Singapore

Portfolio is part of the Penguin Random House group of companies
whose addresses can be found at global.penguinrandomhouse.com

Published by Penguin Random House India Pvt. Ltd
4th Floor, Capital Tower 1, MG Road,
Gurugram 122 002, Haryana, India

First published as *Caravans: Indian Merchants on the Silk Road* in Allen Lane
by Penguin Books India 2015
Published under the present title in Portfolio 2016

ISBN 9780143426165

Typeset in Aldine401 BT by Manipal Digital Systems, Manipal

Printed at Manipal Technologies Limited, India

www.penguin.co.in

MIX
Paper | Supporting
responsible forestry
FSC® C043100

This is a legitimate digitally printed version of the book and therefore might not
have certain extra finishing on the cover.

To
Karen, Madeleine and Abigail

CONTENTS

MAPS

ILLUSTRATIONS

INTRODUCTION

Have we not Indian carpets dark as wine,
Turbans and sashes, gowns and bows and veils,
And broideries of intricate design,
And printed hangings in enormous bales?
—James Elroy Flecker, 'The Golden
Journey to Samarqand'[1]

If you take a right from my house in Delhi and walk a few
hundred yards, you will go past a flirtatious *bhuttawalli*
who serves delicious corn during the monsoons after
roasting it gently on simmering charcoal and sprinkling
it with lemon juice and black salt; twenty yards ahead
on the right sits Verma-ji who cuts my hair with such
care that I no longer have any; after another forty yards,
cross the road and you will find yourself in wondrous
Lodi Gardens. The kings of the forgotten Lodi dynasty

are buried here, their tombs surrounded by sprawling gardens over a hundred acres. The Lodis ruled the Delhi Sultanate from 1451 to 1526 before they lost to the invading armies of Babur, the great Mughal. They were Afghan Pashtuns who got going as horse traders who traversed the pastures between the Indus and Oxus rivers, either leading or robbing caravans across the Hindu Kush mountains en route from India to Central Asia, which were financed most importantly by my Khatri and Arora ancestors based in the city of Multan on the banks of Chenab in undivided Punjab. It was also in Multan that the Lodis' ancestor settled as a horse trader.

For hundreds of years great *qafilas*, 'caravans', travelled through the Hindu Kush mountains of the Western Himalayas, and if you happened to be standing on the Khyber Pass on a bright spring day, you would have seen the astonishing spectacle of thousands of camels carrying rich textiles of all varieties, spices, indigo, sugar, rice and other luxuries, accompanied by hundreds of slaves to be sold in the markets of Bukhara, Tashkent, Isfahan and beyond the Caucasus mountains, as far away as Astrakhan on the mouth of the Volga, eventually reaching Moscow, where they resided in Kitae Gorod, the home of foreign merchants.

On the return journey, the caravans brought tens of thousands of horses bred on the Inner Asian steppe by pastoral nomads for the armies and the aristocracies of India. These Multani traders, many of them Khatri/Aroras, settled down for years together in caravanserais in these exotic towns, where they created a Hindu diaspora and prospered as merchants, goldsmiths, sellers of grain, *saraf*s, bankers who financed the local harvests of agricultural commodities, and even craftsmen such as the ones who helped build Timur's splendid Bibi Khanum mosque in Samarqand.

Hindu Merchants in the Heart of Central Asia

Hindu traders were at the heart of the Central Asian economies—they advanced loans to farmers during the the planting season and purchased the crop in the harvest season, even arranging its transport to the wholesale markets. The local rulers appreciated this valuable service, which helped monetize their economies and facilitated their collection of taxes. In turn, the rulers allowed Indian merchants to live in peace and dignity in their caravanserais, where they observed their own customs and festivals like Holi and Diwali. They had enlisted Brahmins to conduct their ceremonies. The only

Hindu custom that irked conservative Muslim locals was the cremation ceremony, especially the thought of human ashes going up in smoke and polluting the air; consequently, the local Amir of Bukhara would station a military escort in the cremation ground so that resentful locals did not disturb the ceremony.

'The fabulous wealth and unmatched trading skill of the Indians often seemed to excite jealousy of the local people to land them into trouble . . . In Bukhara, it was generally believed that a successful way for a lover to meet the exorbitant demands of his beloved was to locate and plunder the fabulous wealth of a rich Hindu merchant,'[2] writes Muzaffar Alam, a distinguished historian of the Mughal period and an author of a forthcoming volume in this Penguin series. These intrepid traders occasionally married abroad or took local mistresses, but most often they returned home after a decade or so. Before departing, they would convert their hard-earned wealth into *hundi*s, bills of exchange, which were much safer than carrying cash. When they arrived in Multan, they cashed the *hundi*s, cleared their accounts with their Khatri financiers and settled down to a life of ease and prosperity. The more ambitious among them began their own family firms.

Scott Levi has recounted here with much grace and panache the adventurous story of these caravans and caravanserais that thrived over four centuries, from the sixteenth century to the nineteenth century. The expression 'Silk Road' in Levi's subtitle came into vogue only in the 1870s, a romantic notion to describe the latitudinal peddler trade in luxury goods during antiquity between Rome and China. Of course, the reality was more complex and often less than romantic, as Levi explains. Eurasian trade was a conglomeration of overland trade networks that linked all major Eurasian civilizations, including Persia and India, rather than an east–west superhighway, and the commodities were more often bulk goods and livestock rather than luxuries—silk was only a small part of the exchange.

Multan was one of the great trading centres along the Silk Road. It was a trading hub even in ancient India, long before Alexander invaded the city in 326 BCE, when Punjab was the wealthiest province of the Iranian Achaemenid Empire (550–330 CE). Afghanistan was a part of Indian kingdoms from the time of the Mauryas (324–183 BCE) through the reigns of the Hindu Shahis of Kabul in the ninth and tenth centuries CE. Trans-Himalayan trade flourished during the Buddhist expansion in the first to the third centuries CE under the Kushans, who were based in Jalandhar in Punjab and whose kingdom extended all the way to Xinjiang.

After the rise of Islam and the Umayyad conquest in the eighth century, Multan mediated trade between the

Islamic Middle East and Hindu India in medieval times. The Khatri community in Multan rose to prominence during the Delhi Sultanate (1206–1526) as agents and bankers to the nobility in Delhi and dominated the trans-Himalayan trade right through the Mughal Empire until the end of the nineteenth century, when the expanding Russian empire and the Afghan wars of the British brought it to an end. Multani merchants, however, began to shift to Shikarpur in Sind after the decline in Mughal power in the eighteenth century, when conditions deteriorated in the Punjab.

The great contribution of scholars like Scott Levi and Stephen Dale has been to show that the 'Silk Road' did not end with antiquity but continued into the early modern period. The story of the Multani merchant caravans in Central Asia is an extraordinarily successful example. And the excellent scholarship of Ken Pomeranz, Andre Gunder Frank and others has shown that Europeans did *not* dominate world commerce prior to the nineteenth century. Before the Industrial Revolution in the West, India and China were the largest trading nations and controlled more than forty per cent of the world's wealth. The recent rise of China and India in the twenty-first century is gradually restoring the global share of wealth to a historical norm that existed prior to 1750.

Nations Create Wealth through Good Governance

Levi's story teaches many things. One of them is how individuals and nations create wealth. Exchange is natural among human beings. When the state establishes the right conditions, people respond. When governments provide peace, law and order, they fashion a predictable environment for commerce to flourish; when they build infrastructure, business and trade flourish, jobs are created, goods begin to move, taxes grow, and widespread prosperity is the result.

The rulers in India and in Central Asia crafted many of these conditions. The Delhi Sultanate (1206–1526) and the Mughal Empire (1526–1707) ensured reasonable security. Sher Shah Suri, in particular, built shady, tree-lined roads and rest houses for travellers. Akbar, the great Mughal, ruthlessly punished Afghan tribesmen who made a living by robbing caravans. The rulers of the host countries reciprocated. The Uzbek Khans of Bukhara created an official position in the administration, Yasavul-i-Hinduwan, 'Guardian of Hindus', whose job was to look after the welfare of Hindu traders, and help in collecting defaulted loans from among an intolerant Muslim majority. The Persian Safavid Empire (1501–1722) equally protected Hindu merchants and their caravans, also allowing them to practise their customs within their caravanserais among a predominantly Muslim people.

If good governance leads to prosperity, the opposite is also true. Bad, rapacious rulers destroy the wealth of nations. The weakening of Mughal authority in the eighteenth century allowed brutal Nadir Shah to invade India and sack Delhi in 1739. Between 1749 and 1849, the Afghans, Marathas, Sikhs and the British invaded repeatedly the commercial city of Multan. Without the 'peace' provided by the Delhi Sultanate and the Mughal Empire, Multan waned and its merchants moved away to Shikarpur. Levi narrates the poignant story of the death of the once great Multani community in Isfahan—which numbered 25,000 at its peak—because of the simultaneous decline in Safavid power in Iran. Without the peace of the Safavids, Ghilzai tribesman from Afghanistan occupied Isfahan in 1722 and almost decimated the Indian community. A few years later, the infamous Nadir Shah confiscated the wealth of those who remained. In the end, the worst government turned out to be the Russian colonial power, which effectively killed the trans-Himalayan trade over the second half of the nineteenth century.

The role of the state in fostering enterprise and prosperity is a lesson that this 'Story of Indian

Business' has highlighted repeatedly. In antiquity, the *Arthashastra* advised the ruler to protect Vaishyas, 'producers', and tax them mildly—the rightful share of the king is one-sixth or a 15 per cent tax rate; otherwise, both merchants and farmers will move to neighbouring kingdoms and the king will lose his tax base. Kanakalatha Mukund showed how the south Indian kings of the Pandya, Pallava and Chola dynasties created a predictable climate for merchants which contributed to the remarkable trade with Rome and South East Asia. At the beginning of the seventeenth century, the English state made a breakthrough in East–West trade by chartering the East India Company, which may have had negative political consequences for India but it did contribute to prosperity both in England and India. Lakshmi Subramanian underlined the role of the state in her account of Surat's decline and Bombay's rise, which was a direct consequence of waning Mughal power and rising British power in the eighteenth century.

The state can foster the right climate but it has its limits. It is individuals who create wealth through trade and investment, as I elaborate below. When the state in its hubris tries to become an economic actor it invariably fails, a recent and dramatic example being India's License Raj between 1950 and 1991.

An Earlier Globalization
Supplied the Capital

Another lesson from *Caravans* is that capital helps to create wealth. Silver from the Americas began to flood India's markets in the early sixteenth century after Columbus 'discovered' America in 1492 and the Portuguese 'discovered' India soon after in 1498. Portuguese merchants found that Europeans had an insatiable appetite for Indian textiles, spices and other luxuries, but Indians did not particularly want anything from Europe. However, Indians loved gold and silver, and since the books of trade had to be balanced, they were balanced with bullion. Thus, Levi quotes the seventeenth-century French traveller François Bernier: 'Gold and silver, after circulating in every quarter of the globe, come at length to be swallowed up, lost in some measure, in *Hindoustan*'.

Not lost, as Bernier thought—rather it provided the liquidity and capital that financed and multiplied market activity across India in the early modern period. It delivered the means, for example, for Multani merchants to finance the caravan trade across the Himalayas to Central Asia and beyond. After the Europeans 'discovered' India, trade with European companies surged, especially in the seventeenth and eighteenth centuries. Indian textiles, in particular, flourished and Indian textile producers fulfilled a quarter of the world's demand. This created jobs for tens of millions—from farmers who grew cotton and natural dyes, to spinners who turned raw cotton into yarn, to weavers who converted yarn into bolts of cloth, to printers who adorned the cloth, and on to transporters, wholesalers and retailers who sold the final cloth to consumers. Levi shows that the stimulus of Central Asian demand led to the growth of industry and of cities in undivided Punjab. Lahore, Amritsar, Ludhiana, Karnal, Bajwara, Sialkot and others became textile-producing centres. Open borders create wealth for those nations that are not afraid to trade.

Only in the early nineteenth century did this picture change, when the machines of the Industrial Revolution began to supplant handlooms. Indian nationalists make the mistake of believing that the British Raj destroyed the lives of India's textile workers. The truth is that handlooms died around the world and the vast number of workers associated with textiles became a victim of technological obsolescence. Nationalists who clamour for 'swadeshi' and protection forget that trade is not a zero-sum game. Both sides—sellers and buyers—gain. High tariffs and barriers to foreign investment do more harm than good. Protectionist Indians, suffering from the 'East India Company syndrome', are not aware that India derived enormous benefit from the incredible stimulus in European demand. India's own mills would have destroyed handlooms, and indeed, they did just that after the second half of the nineteenth century.

The lesson for today's 'protectionists' is not to learn the wrong lessons from history. Business is dynamic and old technologies constantly die as new ones are born. A nation should not close its borders, as India tragically did from 1950–90, in the pessimistic belief that it could not compete with the world. Scott Levi and the other authors of The Story of Indian Business series teach us that India was historically a great trading nation. Instead of going into its shell in the four decades after Independence, it should have seized opportunities from the dramatic surge in international trade after World War II till the early 1970s. India finally opened up in 1991. When it did, its software and outsourcing industry rose to the occasion and responded brilliantly to the opportunities offered by globalization. It was the stimulus of international demand for software and remote services from India that brought the country new respect, helped lift its economic growth rate and raise millions into the middle class.

Khatris Are an Example of Familial Indian Capitalism

A third piece of the wealth-of-nations puzzle is entrepreneurship. It helps to have individuals, families and communities within a nation who know how to acquire capital; how to conserve it; when to risk it; and how to pass it on to the next generation. India has been long blessed with communities within the Hindu caste system with outstanding entrepreneurial capabilities. Levi has described the Khatris and Aroras, whom Denzil Ibbetson labels Punjab's 'great mercantile castes'. Like the Kayasths, the Khatris were also administrators and had a distinguished record of service in key departments of the Mughal Empire.

To underline the importance of India's commercial communities, this series is publishing a number of books on them. The first is already out, on the formidable Marwaris and authored by the noted authority, Thomas A. Timberg. The Marwaris are also present in Levi's story of the trans-Himalayan trade, but they are bit players, except when individuals occasionally take centre stage in Russian records, such as Marwari Baraev, 'the great Marwari'. Volumes on the Gujarati Kachhis and Tamil Chettiars are underway. Nattukotai Chettiars exerted great economic influence for centuries in south India and South East Asia, while Kachhi (Kutchi) enterprises in coastal Gujarat built a flourishing trade in the eighteenth and nineteenth centuries with the Middle East and Africa. Unlike the land-borne Khatris, the seaborne Chettiars and Kachhis were carried by monsoon winds in the Indian Ocean towards South East Asia, the Middle East and Africa.

India's business communities harnessed the great productive capacity of India. As a result of economic surplus generated in the home market, and with the support of lower costs and the superior quality of Indian textiles, they exercised an inherent competitive advantage. In the conservative Islamic societies of Iran and Central Asia they flourished because of another advantage. Islam forbids usury; hence, even while some Muslims found ways to circumvent that restriction, commercially minded Muslims tended not to focus their efforts on the moneylending trade. Hindu merchants had no such inhibitions, which permitted them to fill a natural economic role that was much in demand. This also became a compelling reason for the Hindu merchant to settle down for years at a time and add to the great Indian diaspora. Not surprisingly, it was commonly said in Central Asia, 'Wherever there is a bazaar, Hindoos are a . . . part of it.'

Levi estimates that the Indian mercantile diaspora numbered as many as 35,000 individuals in the early modern period. Most were Hindus, agents of Indian firms who had left their families behind. They lived with other Indian merchants in Indian caravanserais.

Despite their cultural separation from their hosts, they were able to function both as trans-regional traders as well as suppliers of credit in urban and rural areas. Local rulers protected them because they realized the importance of their financial services.

In non-Islamic societies as well—in East Africa, in East and South East Asia, and in distant Latin America—Indian commercial communities have flourished based on some of these competitive advantages. Today, the Indian diaspora is second in size only to the Chinese. But inward remittances from this diaspora were, in fact, the largest in the five years between 2003 and 2008, and they remain a significant factor in financing India's balance of payments.

Indian capitalism has always been family based, and Khatris are no different. Like other commercial communities, they apprenticed their young early and provided them with rigorous training in technical skills, especially for long-distance trade. When they came of age and were ready to set out on their own, they received venture capital, which they returned after they had made a success. They often became *gumashta*s, agents, and went abroad for seven or eight years, or even longer. Because they belonged either to the extended family or at least to the same sub-caste of the Multani firm, its *sah*s, directors or principals, had a hold on their investment. *Gumashta*s left their families behind, which also deterred them from absconding abroad with the firm's capital.

Levi reiterates an important lesson that we learned from Timberg's *The Marwaris*: reputation is at the heart of the Indian family firm. The directors needed to trust their agents. If the agent cheated or did not keep his word or swindled a customer, it tarnished the firm's reputation. Word spread quickly that the firm's other agents were also not to be trusted. Hence, firms preferred to recruit agents from their extended family or sub-caste and invested substantial energies in their training from a very young age. All this ensured the firm's reputation and built trust, which are universally at the heart of the market's morality.

Trade Influences Ideology

Another lesson from *Caravans* is one that Karl Marx also taught: economic circumstances affect culture and ideology. Not surprisingly, the vigorous Khatri/Arora trade in Central Asia influenced the new religion of Sikhism that was born in the Punjab around this time. Many of the Khatri/Arora families turned to Sikhism. The historians Chetan Singh and Muzaffar Alam have both pointed out that some of the language in the passages of the early Sikh scriptures, especially the Guru Granth Saheb, is the language of commerce.

> The true guru is the merchant; devotees are his peddlers; the Lord's name is the stock of capital; to enshrine the truth is to keep its accounts.[3]

Again:

> Without capital, the trader looks about in vain on the four continents. He knows not that his capital lies buried within himself.
> Without merchandise, he grieves; the false are deceived.
> He who has the knowledge of the jewel within himself reaps profit,
> And gathers his goods at home and fulfills himself.
> Trade with the true traders and dwell on the Lord through the Guru's words.[4]

The Story of Indian Business

The various lessons that we can learn from this book— the role of good governance, the stimulating effect of international capital, the role of trust and reputation in the business life—are the sorts of issues which have engaged the authors of our unique multi-volume history of Indian business. *Caravans: Indian Merchants on the Silk Road* is the seventh volume in Penguin's The Story of Indian Business series. This series attempts to mine great ideas in business and economics that have shaped commerce in the Indian subcontinent while, entertaining us with the romance of the high seas or adventures in the bazar.

Leading contemporary scholars closely examine historical texts, inscriptions and records, and interpret them in a lively, sharp and authoritative manner for the intelligent reader who may have no prior background in the field. Each slender volume offers an enduring perspective on business enterprise in the past, avoiding the pitfall of simplistically cataloguing a set of lessons for today. The value of the exercise is to promote a longer-term sensibility in the reader in order to understand the material bases for our present human condition and think sensibly about our economic future. Taken together, the series as a whole celebrates the ideal captured in the Sanskrit word *artha*.

The series began with Tom Trautmann's interpretation for our times of the renowned treatise on the science of wealth, *Arthashastra*, which was authored almost two thousand years ago and is considered the world's first manual in political economy. Kanakalatha Mukund took us south in the next volume, *Merchants of Tamilakam*, to a beguiling world when a ship from Rome used to touch one of the ports of south India daily. Mukund has reconstructed this world, to the end of the Chola Empire, by drawing on the epics *Silappadikaram* and *Manimekalai* and other historical materials. Next, we jumped centuries to Tirthankar Roy's radiant account of the East India Company, which taught us, among other things, how much the modern multinational corporation is a child of a company that is reviled even today in India. Our fourth volume hopped again to the late eighteenth century, to the decline of Surat and the rise of Bombay. In it, Lakshmi Subramanian sets the stage for the ups and downs in the adventurous lives of the *Three Merchants of Bombay: Trawadi Arjunji Nathji, Jamsetjee Jeejeebhoy and Premchand Roychand*. Arshia Sattar recounts in the fifth volume the brilliant adventures of *The Mouse Merchant* and other tales based on the *Kathasaritsagara*, the *Panchatantra* and other sources.

In the future lies a veritable feast. Three more books will cover the ancient and early medieval periods: Gregory Schopen will present the *Business Model of*

Early Buddhist Monasticism based on the *Mulasarvastivada Vinaya*; Donald Davis will raise contemporary issues in the area of commercial and business law based on medieval commentaries by authors such as Vacaspati Mishra and Chandeshvara on the voluminous *Dharmashastras*. Next, the celebrated Sanjay Subrahmanyam and Muzaffar Alam will transport us into the world of sultans, shopkeepers and portfolio capitalists in Mughal India. Chhaya Goswami will dive deep with Jerry Rao into the Indian Ocean to recount the tale of Kachchhi enterprise in the triangle formed by Mandvi, Muscat and Zanzibar. Raman Mahadevan will describe the Nattukottai Chettiars' search for fortune. Omkar Goswami will give us the definitive account of the managing agencies. Finally, Medha Kudaisiya will round out the series by breathing life into the historic 'Bombay Plan', recording a story of betrayal related to an economic plan for India drawn by eminent industrialists in 1944–45.

*

India's power has always been 'soft', not expressed through conquest and military dominance, but in the export of ideas and goods. Among goods, textiles and spices were a perennial draw and they helped change culinary tastes and clothing habits around the world. In antiquity, the white flowing togas of upper-class Romans were made from Indian cloth. As were the white turbans of the Central Asian Turks: 'The Indians doe bring fine whites which the Tartars doe roll about their heads,' observed a traveller to Central Asia in 1558, whom Scott Levi quotes here. Around this time Europeans began to wear underwear because they discovered soft and affordable Indian cloth that reached them by sea via the East India Company. It was mostly one-way traffic, however, as Indians were not much interested, as I already pointed out, in what the Europeans made—that is, until the Industrial Revolution in the nineteenth century. The only way to balance the trade was with gold and silver. Thus, a French monk who visited Persia compared the Safavid Empire of Iran to a caravanserai with two doors. Gold and silver entered from the western door and exited from the eastern door to India, 'where all the money in the Universe is unloaded as if it into an abyss.' Even in the twenty-first century, India seems to be an 'abyss' of the world's gold. In 2013, a surge in gold imports was one of the main reasons for the crisis in India's current account, which only corrected itself with the imposition of gold controls.

Gurcharan Das
New Delhi

PREFACE

Why Central Asia?

My interest in India's historical relationship with Central Asia dates back more than two decades. During the summer of 1988, I participated in an intensive course in Hindi at the Landour Language School in Mussoorie, a serene and beautiful hill station in Uttar Pradesh (UP). Midway through the course I took a short break for an undergraduate research trip to the inner-Himalayan pilgrimage sites of Yamunotri and Gangotri. I returned to the United States fascinated with India, and yearning for more. A considerable amount of coursework and three years later, I had earned a bachelor's degree in South Asian studies and begun preparations to return to South Asia, this time to Lahore, in order to participate in the Berkeley Urdu Language Program in Pakistan.

I spent much of the 1991–92 academic year in Pakistan, living with a very kind family and studying Urdu. On those occasions when I was able to take a break from my studies, I would leave Lahore behind to explore locations in both Pakistan and India. On one such trip, in early 1992, I made my way to the Islamabad airport. As I approached the terminal my attention was drawn upwards, to a large banner flapping in the wind above the entrance. The banner was pale blue, white and green, and it announced the commencement of an Uzbekistan Airways flight connecting Islamabad with Tashkent, the capital of the newly independent Republic of Uzbekistan. I was aware that the Soviet Union had collapsed just a few months earlier, but everything beyond the civil war raging in Afghanistan seemed distant. This was my first encounter with evidence that the Central Asian world to the north had changed. I knew very little about Tashkent and Uzbekistan, but that banner piqued my interest in Central Asia, a region that now seemed much closer.

As I continued my studies in Lahore, I began to find echoes of the strong historical bond shared by the people of South and Central Asia. As my skills in Urdu improved I began to encounter Turkic words that had made their way into the Urdu language (including the word 'Urdu' itself). On a camel trek through the

Cholistan Desert, near Bahawalpur, I visited several shrines belonging to Sufis of past generations, and was hosted by the current patriarch of one Sufi dynastic family. I found that the Naqshbandiyya and other Sufi orders that had at various times become popular and had a large following in South Asia had their roots in Central Asia. And as I explored Lahore and the magnificent architecture of the Mughal era, I learned more about the Mughal emperors, descendants of the great Central Asian conqueror Tamerlane, and the earlier Turko-Afghan rulers of the Delhi Sultanate.

It was clear that these two regions shared a close historical relationship, but my analysis of the scholarship available to me at the time and my experience in Pakistan suggested that the relationship had been unidirectional. Conquering armies from Central Asia brought their language and religious traditions into South Asia; I found no evidence of a corresponding movement of people or merchandise emanating from what appeared to be a passive India. This did not sit right with me. I hypothesized that if I were to make my way to Central Asia, I would find evidence of Indian influences beyond the Hindu Kush. After returning to the United States, I began graduate school and worked to design a programme that would enable me to conduct my PhD dissertation research on this topic in Uzbekistan.

For several years I studied Uzbek and Persian and in 1995, I made my first trip to Uzbekistan, a short preliminary research visit of just one month. In Tashkent, I met with a number of scholars, some of whom have become close friends over the years, and I learned much about what lay ahead for me. I was pleased to find that the archives of Uzbekistan hold a wealth of manuscripts and other materials that would be invaluable to my research. I also learned that during the 1950s and 1960s several Soviet-era scholars had directed attention to Indo–Central Asian relations in the medieval and early modern eras. And I found that the majority of the scholarship from the Soviet era, as well as the catalogues to the archives, were available only in Russian. I returned again to the United States and immediately enrolled in an intensive Russian course so that I could return to Uzbekistan for a much longer research trip, which took place in 1996–97. The material I present in this book is the culmination of that research.

There are many people to whom I owe a debt of gratitude for encouraging and facilitating the production of this book. First and foremost is Gurcharan Das, whose vision for the importance of Indian business history in the larger context of modern Indian society is truly inspiring. Among my many friends and colleagues in Tashkent who helped me access restricted collections and find my way through the manuscripts, I am deeply indebted to the late eminent historian of sixteenth-century Central Asia Roziya Mukminova, and my dear friend Ghulom Karimov who passed away as I prepared this volume, as well as Marina Kutina, Akram Khabibullaev, and Rano Magrufova, the most generous and resourceful librarian anyone could hope to encounter. In my graduate programme at the University of Wisconsin-Madison, I remain grateful to my graduate adviser, André Wink, as well as Uli Schamiloglu and Anatoly Khazanov for their guidance and continued interest in my research. And I am similarly grateful to a number of colleagues in the scholarly community whose work has had a direct and profound influence on my own. The list is long, and I hope I can be forgiven for mentioning only Stephen Dale, Claude Markovits, Muzaffar Alam and Surendra Gopal.

I thank the Social Science Research Council and the American Councils for International Education for their support, both financial and logistical. I am grateful to Stephen Grantham and Mitchell Albert at Garnet Publishing (UK) Ltd for their generous permission to reproduce here six photographs of Indian merchants in Bukhara from the *Bukhara* volume in Garnet's series

Caught in Time: Great Photographic Archives (Reading, UK, 1993), edited by Vitaly Naumkin and compiled by Andrei G. Nedvetsky. And I thank Patricia Rader and Gaby van Rietschoten at E.J. Brill for their support and for granting me permission to revisit my published work, *The Indian Diaspora in Central Asia and Its Trade, 1550–1900* (Leiden, 2002), and present it here in a distilled and updated format. Finally, for their love and support I thank my wife, Karen Spierling, and our two wonderful daughters, Madeleine and Abigail Levi. They add a richness to life that is beyond words, and I dedicate this volume to them.

I have revised the conclusions that I lay out in this volume to reflect the way my thinking has changed over the years. But they are also in many ways products of that original research, and a testament to the fact that my initial hypothesis was not misguided. While I did not yet know the depths of what awaited me in Uzbekistan, readers of this volume will find that Indians were anything but passive in their relations with their neighbours to the north and west.

TIMELINE

977–1186   Ghaznavids become independent of the Samanids in Bukhara; establish a Turkic-Muslim power centered in Afghanistan, stretching far into Iran and India

998–1030   Mahmud of Ghazna institutionalizes earlier practice of raiding India for slaves and treasure; leads seventeen campaigns, demolishes temples, and exports tens—perhaps even hundreds—of thousands of slaves to markets in Afghanistan and Central Asia

1150–1215   Ghurids sack Ghazna and assert authority over territories stretching from eastern Iran across northern India; raiding and

	looting of Indian temples and settlements continue as under the Ghaznavids
1206–1555	Delhi Sultanate period of Indian history
1206–90	First of the Delhi Sultanates, the Shamsi Slave Kings, former Ghurid military slaves, assume authority in India; widespread enslavement and exportation continue
1266–87	Reign of Sultan Balban, during which for the first time Barani identifies Multanis as professional moneylenders
1290–1320	Khaljis assume authority in Delhi and establish their own sultanate; raids extend deep into the Deccan
1296–1316	Reign of 'Ala' al-Din Khalji, during which Barani identifies Multanis as large-scale moneylenders and wholesale dealers in textiles
1320–1414	Tughluq dynasty assumes authority in Delhi

1336–1405	Lifetime of the Central Asian Turkic conqueror Timur, or Tamerlane
1398	Timur launches an invasion of India, defeats Tughluqid army and sacks Delhi; wealth and many thousands of slaves dispatched to his capital of Samarqand
1409–47	Shah Rukh succeeds his father, Timur; moves the capital to Herat and places his son, Ulugh Bek, in Samarqand
1414–51	Delhi Sultanate falls to the Sayyid dynasty of Khizr Khan, former governor of Multan; claims to rule in the name of the Timurid ruler Shah Rukh
1451–1526	Lodi Afghans overthrow the ineffective leadership of the Sayyid dynasty
1498	Vasco da Gama leads a small Portuguese armada to Calicut, in India, by sea
1500	Samarqand is conquered by the Uzbeks under Muhammad Shibani Khan; the

young Timurid, Zahir al-Din Muhammad
Babur, is forced to flee to Afghanistan

1500–99   Shibanid Uzbeks rule in Central Asia

1501–1722   Safavids rule in Iran: first from Tabriz,
then Qazvin, and then Isfahan

1526   Babur's armies defeat Ibrahim Lodi at the
Battle of Panipat, establishing the Timurid
'Mughal' (in Central Asia, 'Baburid') Empire

1526–1858   Mughals rule in India

1540   Afghan ruler Sher Shah (or Sher Khan,
d. 1545) defeats Babur's son and heir,
Humayun, at Kanauj; Humayun seeks refuge
with the Safavid Shah Tahmasp in Iran

1540–55   Suri dynasty interrupts Humayun's reign
as the final Delhi Sultanate; dedicates
considerable resources to building and
maintaining roads, caravanserais, and other
commercial institutions linking India with
markets to the north and west

1552	Russian Empire annexes the Khanate of Kazan on the upper Volga River
1555	Humayun returns to India and restores Mughal authority
1555	Muscovy Company is chartered in England in order to pursue trade with Asian markets
1556	Humayun dies, leaving the empire to his young son, Akbar (b. 1542)
1556	Russian Empire annexes the Khanate of Astrakhan; Russian control extends down the Volga River to the Caspian Sea
1558	Anthony Jenkinson, of the English Muscovy Company, travels the Volga en route to Bukhara; his report focuses on commercial potential in the region and mentions Indian merchants in Shibanid Bukhara
1559	First known reference of Multanis in Bukhara

1561–98   Abdullah Khan II rules in Bukhara, first under the authority of his father, Iskandar, and from 1583 as the official Khan

1572   Abdullah Khan II sends his first embassy to Emperor Akbar, advocating for friendly relations and regular commercial and diplomatic exchanges between the two realms

1588–92   Judicial record, the *Majmu'a-i Wathaiq*, records activities of Multani merchants in Shibanid Samarqand

1599–1747 Uzbek Shibanids are replaced by the similarly Uzbek Ashtarkhanid (or Janid, or Toqay-Timurid) dynasty of Bukharan Khans

1600   English East India Company is chartered

1601   Dutch East India Company (V.O.C.) is chartered

1637   Adam Olearius reports 12,000 Indians living in the Safavid capital of Isfahan

1638   Earliest record of Indian merchants reaching the city of Astrakhan, in Russia; Indians travel up the Volga in later years, reaching even Moscow and St Petersburg

1646–47   Mughal Emperor Shah Jahan launches a failed invasion of Balkh; Uzbek-Mughal diplomatic relations disrupted, but then re-established under Aurangzeb (r. 1658–1707) and Abd al-Aziz Khan (r. 1645–1681)

1666–67   French traveller Jean Chardin estimates 20,000 'Multanis' living in Safavid Iran

1707   Aurangzeb dies; Mughal Empire rapidly decentralizes

1722   Ghilzai Afghans invade Safavid territory and occupy Isfahan; Afghans extort wealth of Hindu merchants in Isfahan

1735   Russians encourage Indians to bypass Iran and shift their trade interests eastwards from Astrakhan to Orenburg; the primary trade route to reach Russia from the south now passes through Bukhara

1736   Safavid military commander, Nadir
            Tahmasp Quli Khan, overthrows the shah
            and usurps regal authority as Nadir Shah;
            devastates Hindu communities across Iran

1737   Nadir Shah invades Central Asia

1739   Nadir Shah invades Mughal India and sacks
            Delhi

1740   Nadir Shah invades Bukhara a second
            time; city is protected but his troops
            pillage the countryside

1747   Nadir Shah is assassinated; Indians begin
            to return to Persian markets

1747   Ahmad Khan of the Afghan Abdali tribe
            assumes authority over Nadir Shah's
            eastern territories and rules as Ahmad
            Shah Durrani until his death in 1772;
            Durranis encourage Indian merchants to
            settle in their territory

1747   Leadership of the Uzbek Manghit tribe
            usurps authority from the Chinggisid

Ashtarkhanids in Bukhara; Manghit Amirs retain puppet khans until 1785

1749–1848 City of Multan suffers repeated invasions and occupations; many Multanis elect to relocate to Shikarpur, in Durrani-controlled Sind

1757 Battle of Plassey; marks the rise of British rule in India

1758–59 Qing conquest of Xinjiang

1799–1876 Khanate of Khoqand established in Ferghana Valley; expansion of trade and irrigation agriculture draws substantial number of Indian merchants into that region for the first time

1832 British agent Alexander Burnes travels to Bukhara, reports that Indian merchants there enjoyed the state's protection and abundant commercial opportunities

1839–42 First Anglo-Afghan War

1858   East India Company dissolved and last
            Mughal emperor dismissed; British
            Crown rule established in India

1863   Hungarian scholar Arminius Vámbéry
            travels to Bukhara, estimates the city to
            be home to a thriving community of 500
            Indian merchants

1865   Russian army enters Tashkent and takes
            the city

1865–1918   Russia expands control in Central Asia;
            Tashkent, Samarqand and the Ferghana
            Valley are colonized; Bukhara and Khiva
            are reduced to protectorates

1877   Russian governor general Konstantin
            von Kaufman issues a circular severely
            limiting Indian commercial activities in
            Russian Turkestan; results in large-scale
            withdrawal of Indian merchants from
            Russian territory

1878–80   Second Anglo-Afghan War

1914–18   World War I

1917–22   October Revolution begins in St Petersburg, continues as Russian Civil War

1922   Soviet Union established; Bukharan and Khivan Khanates dissolved; new Soviet Socialist Republics of Central Asia established; residual Indian commercial presence in Central Asia ended

1939–45   World War II

1947   Social unrest associated with Indian independence and partition brings an end to the centuries-long Indian commercial presence in Afghanistan

PROLOGUE

In the year 1500, the Chinggisid Uzbek ruler Muhammad Shibani Khan led an invasion of Central Asia and forced Zahir al-Din Muhammad Babur, the last Timurid to rule in the ancestral capital of Samarqand, to flee his homeland and seek refuge in Afghanistan. Babur led a small entourage of loyal followers southwards to Kabul. While he dearly missed the comforts and climate of his Central Asian homeland, Babur was attracted by India's much larger and wealthier population. In 1526, he defeated Ibrahim Lodi at the Battle of Panipat and initiated a new Timurid state in India: the Mughal Empire (1526–1707/1858). At roughly the same time as the Uzbeks pushed Babur out of Samarqand, another Turkic dynasty with roots in the Inner Asian steppe was consolidating control in Iran— the Shia Muslim Safavids (1501–1722/36).

In terms of demographics, there were a number of significant differences among the Mughal, Uzbek and Safavid states. Whereas the Mughals were a predominantly Muslim ruling elite governing a much larger non-Muslim population, the Uzbeks and Safavids were Muslim nobility ruling over considerably smaller, and primarily Muslim, populaces. Additionally, while the climates of Iran and Central Asia are dry by comparison, Mughal India's rich soils and wet climate could support an agricultural civilization that exceeded the combined population of the Safavid and Uzbek realms by a factor of ten. This gave Indian producers a profound advantage in the production of cotton, grains and other agricultural goods, contributing to India's much larger regional economy. We will see, however, that climatic factors were very much in Central Asia's favour when it came to the breeding of horses, many tens of thousands of which were transported to Indian markets each year to be used for military or other purposes.

From the middle of the sixteenth century, several factors contributed to a general intensification of Mughal India's commercial relationship with the Uzbek and Safavid states. Arguably the most important of these is that rulers recognized that they shared a common interest in promoting trade by investing in their commercial infrastructures, working to ensure safe passage through their trade routes, and welcoming foreign traders into their realms. Rulers occasionally exchanged embassies to address important matters. But they also equipped caravan traders with official letters requesting permission to enter neighbouring realms, and when foreign merchants arrived at their borders they reciprocated in kind. The legendary wealth and opulence of the Mughal court drew Muslim elite from Central Asia and Iran to India in large numbers, and their correspondence with distant family and colleagues further linked these regions in an informal network of information exchange.

There were, of course, significant differences among these states. Unlike the Mughals and Safavids, the Uzbeks in the north had only recently departed the steppe for the southern sedentary zone in Central Asia. By the middle of the sixteenth century, as Samarqand diminished from its status as a Timurid capital, Bukhara rose as the region's chief political and commercial centre. When the Shibanid dynasty ended in 1599, leadership shifted to another Uzbek lineage—that boasted a Chinggisid bloodline—of Bukharan Khans who had come southwards from Astrakhan following the Russian conquest of that city in 1556. The Ashtarkhanids (also referred to as Janids and Toqay-Timurids) ruled until 1747, after which the Uzbek Manghit Amirs assumed power in Bukhara, dismissing their final Chinggisid puppet khan in 1785.

Over the course of the eighteenth century, another Uzbek tribe, the Ming (of no relation to the Chinese Ming dynasty, 1368–1644), gradually assumed power in the Ferghana Valley, Babur's birthplace, and in 1740 established the city of Khoqand as their new capital. Soon thereafter, in 1758–59, Qing armies conquered neighbouring Xinjiang. By officially recognizing a subordinate status to the Qing, the Uzbek Ming gained access to Chinese markets. Merchants from Ferghana made their way eastwards, Khoqand prospered and, by the end of the century, the Ming ruled the entire valley and established a new Uzbek state. In the first decades of the nineteenth century, the Khanate of Khoqand (1799–1876) expanded to the north and west, conquering Tashkent and reaching far into the steppe. Khoqand benefited greatly from the expansion of irrigation agriculture and efforts to capitalize on commercial relations with Qing markets to the east and Russian markets along the Orenburg Line to the north. These same factors drew large numbers of Indian merchants to the valley for the first time.

By the middle of the nineteenth century, Russian armies had conquered southwards to the limits of the steppe. The Russians entered Tashkent in 1865, and soon thereafter moved on to Samarqand and the Ferghana Valley. Khoqand was defeated and initially designated a protectorate. In 1876, the Khanate was liquidated and the Ferghana Valley was incorporated into Russian colonial Turkestan. The Bukharan Amirate and Khivan Khanate limped on as protectorates until the end of the Revolution, when they were both terminated and folded into the new Soviet Union.

Farther to the south, the Safavids set themselves apart as a Shia Muslim state surrounded by Sunni Muslim Mughal, Uzbek and Ottoman domains. Highlighting this confessional distinction, in the later sixteenth century, the Shibanid ruler Abdullah Khan II sought to convince Emperor Akbar to join him in a campaign to bring an end to the Safavids and divide the spoils between them. Although the Mughals and Safavids launched recurrent small-scale campaigns against each other—over the years Qandahar changed hands a dozen times—Emperor Akbar declined to upset a profitable status quo to join the Uzbeks. The Safavid state persisted into the eighteenth century. In the end, the Ghilzai Afghan invasion of 1722 inflicted critical damage to the Safavid government and economy. The Turkmen commander Nadir Tahmasp Quli Khan forced the Afghans from Safavid territory, but he then overthrew the final shah in 1736 and usurped authority for himself as Nadir Shah. Over the next decade, Nadir Shah's armies invaded India, Central Asia and the Caucasus. The quarter century from the Afghan invasion of 1722 until Nadir Shah was assassinated by one of his subordinate commanders in 1747 marks the most disruptive period in the long history of the Indian merchant diaspora.

During the late eighteenth and nineteenth centuries, prosperity returned to the Indians in Iran under the Zand and Qajar dynasties, as it did in Afghanistan under the Durranis. Taking over Nadir Shah's eastern territories in 1747, Ahmad Shah Durrani and his successors extended their control over the trade routes connecting India with Central Asia. The Durranis protected commercial traffic, and, setting aside Nadir Shah's parasitic policies, they once again welcomed Hindu merchants to pass through and establish settlements within their territories.

Over the second half of the eighteenth century, a clear distinction appeared in the composition of these Indian communities. Nadir Shah's 1739 sack of Delhi had accelerated the collapse of Mughal authority, which began to deteriorate almost immediately following Aurangzeb's death in 1707. During the century from 1749–1849, the city of Multan suffered invasions from

Afghans, Sikhs, Marathas and then the British. During this time, large numbers of Multanis chose to abandon their home in favour of Shikarpur, in Durrani-controlled Sind, where they were joined in their commercial ventures abroad by other commercially minded Sindi communities. Shikarpuris were found active throughout virtually all of the cities and villages in Central Asia until late in the nineteenth century; they similarly remained active throughout Afghanistan until 1947, when the trauma of Partition effectively dislocated their commercial networks in the region.

1. INTRODUCTION

Since long before recorded history, traders have
assembled caravans to transport merchandise between
the South Asian communities and their neighbours to
the north and west. Archaeological evidence indicates
that by the third millennium BCE, inhabitants of the
Indus Valley participated in sustained commercial
exchanges with the peoples of Mesopotamia and the
ancient settlements to the north of the Oxus. Over the
centuries, as populated regions grew in number and in
size, the caravan trade connecting them expanded. By
the beginning of the Common Era, Indian merchants
had developed an elaborate network that facilitated their
movement across what could be harsh and dangerous
terrain. This included financing the excavation of wells,
the planting of trees to provide relief for travellers, and

the construction of roads, bridges and caravanserais. Indian merchants financed religious institutions as well, and the Buddhist art and architecture that many favoured at the time gradually made its way along the trade routes through Afghanistan to Central Asia. Along with its iconography, the Buddhist faith also made its way from India to Central Asia, and then eastwards to China, where local populations received it warmly.

Pointing to the spread of Buddhism along the trade routes, some scholars have sought to link India with the 'Silk Road' trade, the fabled overland commercial network generally considered to have emerged in the second century BCE, during China's Han dynasty (206 BCE—220 CE). At the outset, it is important to dismiss the Eurocentric notions that the Silk Road was a premodern superhighway of sorts, set up to link Chinese production centres with European markets. In addition to being a gross oversimplification, this belief places an exaggerated emphasis on European markets, and distorts the totality of overland Eurasian trade. It also obscures the complexities of the multiple overlapping networks that spanned the Eurasian interior, and it reduces the Indian role in Eurasian trade to a minor tributary of an imagined trunk road that stretched from the Mediterranean to the Han capital of Chang'an, modern Xi'an.

India has been an important participant in overland Eurasian trade since antiquity. As this volume will seek to demonstrate, this would remain the case even through the early modern era, as European merchants made their way to India by sea and returned with ships heavily laden with Indian textiles, dyes, spices and other merchandise. Early modern European consumers no doubt eagerly awaited the arrival of Asian merchandise at European port cities. But by no means did the arrival of European traders in the Indian Ocean signal a decline in the caravan trade. These very same commodities were also strapped on to pack animals and transported in bulk overland to consumers in the many other markets elsewhere in Eurasia. The Eurasian caravan trade continued into the twentieth century, when the well-trodden paths of packed earth gave way to rail lines, with steam locomotives replacing pack animals as the most efficient means to transport bulk goods across great distances overland.

On the face of it, the notion that India's trade with Central Asia grew substantially during the early modern era may appear counterintuitive. Indeed, a school of thought from within the field of Central Asian history argues that, from the seventeenth century, the growing monopoly that the Dutch and English East India Companies enjoyed in the movement of Asian goods to

Europe resulted in the demise of the overland caravan trade. This is presumed to have removed Central Asia to a peripheral position in global trade, sending the region into a lengthy period of economic isolation and abject decline from which it would recover only in the years following Russian colonization.[1] But our discussion here will show that the caravan trade did continue, and Indian merchants in particular remained fully entrenched in Central Asia even to the end of the nineteenth century.

Warfare and other political crises periodically disrupted commercial traffic, but the long periods of stability during the Mughal era brought a rhythm to the movement of people across the frontier. Even when one factor or another might disrupt that rhythm, Indian merchants were sufficiently innovative to continue in their ventures by finding new routes to move merchandise between regions, or redirecting their interests to more stable and predictable markets.

On the one hand, this study aims to analyse the nature of the caravan trade that connected early modern India and Central Asia —identifying the principal goods that merchants moved between regions, and how they conducted their trade. On the other, it is also a story of the people involved: the many tens of thousands of Multanis and Shikarpuris, as well as Marwaris,

Sikhs and others who made their way the full distance from India to Bukhara and Samarqand in modern Uzbekistan, Isfahan in Iran, Baku in Azerbaijan, the Russian port city of Astrakhan at the mouth of the Volga, and beyond. For more than three centuries, these Indians orchestrated a vast commercial network that stretched from north-western India across much of Eurasia.

This volume begins by introducing the dynamics of the caravan trade, and the role that the states played in encouraging trans-regional commercial exchanges. One of the primary indicators of the continued vitality of early modern Central Asia and its strong economic relationship with India is the presence of thousands of Indian merchants inhabiting caravanserais and, in some places, their own quarters in cities and villages across virtually all of sedentary Central Asia. The next two chapters will turn attention to the merchants themselves, agents of caste-based family firms commonly referred to as Multanis because of their association with firms centralized in that north-west Indian city (now in Pakistan). Chapter two will place these merchants in their South Asian context and trace the history of the Multani family firms to the thirteenth century, when they first appear in historical sources. A number of factors contributed to their medieval development, arguably the most important of which was the sustained effort of the Turko-Afghan Delhi Sultanate nobility to encourage the monetization of the Indian economy in order to facilitate their collection of revenue in cash. At the same time, the Delhi Sultanate linked Indian markets with those in the north and west, and this also offered the Multanis attractive new opportunities to develop commercial interests beyond the boundaries of the subcontinent.

The Multani firms continued to flourish as the Mughal emperors maintained policies similar to those of the earlier Delhi Sultans, and European traders injected an even greater amount of precious metals—originally extracted from the Americas, Japan and elsewhere—into the Indian Ocean economy. Growth begat competition, and, as we will see, this motivated the Multani firms to seek out new opportunities by diversifying their commercial portfolios geographically. Already by the middle of the sixteenth century, senior Multani investors began to dispatch agents to Bukhara, Samarqand and other markets far beyond the Hindu Kush where they could take advantage of similar commercial opportunities in a less competitive setting. Our discussion will examine the remarkably diverse portfolios of trade and moneylending investments that these Indian firms boasted long before the European companies arrived in the Indian Ocean. One hopes this will lead those who have looked to Europe for the roots of Asian capitalism to rethink their basic assumptions about Indian business history.

Chapter three illustrates the Indian merchants' modus operandi, as they expanded their impressively integrated commercial network to distant markets, and the relationships that emerged between the Indians and their host states and societies in Central Asia. Indian merchants maintained thriving communities in Central Asia despite the fact that the vast majority of the Indian population consisted of Hindu merchants in Muslim states, people technically unprotected by Islamic law.

That said, the Indians' shrewd moneylending methods did indeed lead many of their Central Asian neighbours to view them as exploitative usurers. Still, a few notable exceptions aside, Indian merchants enjoyed the steadfast protection of their host governments. This is partly because Indian merchants were widely respected as large-scale trans-regional traders whose fortitude, technical knowledge and commercial networks were recognized as exceptionally valuable to the regional economy. More important, however, were the contributions Indian merchants made to their hosts' efforts to monetize their own economies. In Central Asia, and wherever else they were found, the Indian family firms and their agents wielded the strength and resources of the Indian economy as an engine for early modern agricultural and industrial production.

The next three chapters shift the focus away from the traders, and towards the merchandise that they dealt in during this period. Each year Indian merchants dispatched thousands of camels to Central Asian markets, loaded principally with textiles, but also with indigo and other dyes, spices, sugar, rice and more. Large numbers of enslaved Indians were forced to march alongside these caravans. They too were sold in Central Asian markets, and few ever returned to their homeland.

In exchange, Central Asian caravan traders supplied India with produce, principally the fruit for which the region was famous, but also paper, leather goods and wool acquired from their nomadic neighbours in the steppe, and fine silks and porcelains from China. By far, however, the horses bred by pastoral nomads in the Inner Asian steppe represented the region's greatest export to India, China and Russia. Each year, Central Asian and Afghan horse traders led tens of thousands of Central Asian horses across mountain passes in the Hindu Kush. At the same time, traders moved additional numbers southwards to Hormuz and other Persian Gulf ports, where the animals were loaded on to ships and delivered to Indian markets by sea.

Such an analysis might leave one with the impression that the caravan trade defined India's commercial relationship with Central Asia, and that its depth was a factor of the amount of merchandise that caravan traders moved from market to distant market at any given point in time. But our study demonstrates that this is only part of a larger picture, which includes the diverse commercial interests of the many thousands of Indian merchants who took up residence in Central Asia and mediated the majority of the commercial interactions between these two regions from the middle of the sixteenth century through the turn of the twentieth century.

The final chapter of this volume will survey the Indians' early modern commercial network, especially as it pertains to Central Asia but also to Afghanistan, Iran and even Russia. It will illustrate the flexibility of the Indians' commercial system, as they chose to abandon certain markets in favour of emerging opportunities elsewhere. It will demonstrate that Indian merchants retained a dominant commercial position in Central Asia even into the Russian colonial era in the late nineteenth century. And it will examine the Russian colonial policies that undermined the Indians' interests in the region and, ultimately, brought an end to the caravan trade that had for so long connected India with Central Asia.

2. MERCHANTS AND THE STATE

Hindustanis call everything outside of Hindustan 'Khurasan', just as the Arabs call everything not Arab 'Ajam'. On the land route between Hindustan and Khurasan are two trading depots, Kabul and Kandahar. Caravans come to Kabul from Fergana, Turkistan, Samarkand, Bukhara, Balkh, Hissar, and Badakhshan. From Khurasan, they go to Kandahar. As the entrepôt between Hindustan and Khurasan, this province is an excellent mercantile center. Merchants who go to Cathay and Anatolia do no greater business. Every year seven, eight, or ten thousand horses come to Kabul. From Hindustan, caravans of ten, fifteen, twenty thousand pack animals bring slaves, textiles, rock sugar, refined sugar, and spices. Many Kabul merchants would not be satisfied with a 300 to 400 percent profit. Goods from Khurasan, Iraq,

Anatolia, and China can be found in Kabul, which is the
principal depot for Hindustan.[1]
—Zahir al-Din Muhammad Babur, c. 1504

It is no surprise that Babur, the founder of the Mughal Empire, took an immediate interest in the commercial economy of Kabul. Born into the Timurid royal family in Central Asia and schooled in governance from an early age, Babur was acutely aware that ruling elites and caravan traders shared a symbiotic relationship: simply put, they needed each other. Pushed from his native Central Asia to Kabul, he knew that his future and the future of his line would depend upon the prosperity of his subjects. Towards that goal, he needed to encourage traders from India and elsewhere to keep his subjects supplied with merchandise not available in his newly conquered *vilayat*. He stood to profit handsomely if he could retain Kabul's position as a commercial hub along active trade routes connecting India with Central Asia.

From their perspective, caravan traders depended upon Babur, as they did all rulers, to provide a safe and predictable environment in which to trade and to travel through, en route to other markets. The symbiotic nature of this relationship took other forms as well. Historical sources provide abundant references to rulers taking advances from merchants in order to finance military campaigns, for example.

While a peaceful and predictable environment was the norm, for one reason or another the equilibrium of this symbiotic relationship was occasionally upset. Simple thieves and predatory tribes posed a persistent threat to caravan traders. Should rulers fail to provide a safe environment in their cities and on their trade routes, merchants would abandon their markets and redirect their interests towards other more predictable environments. If, in need of resources, rulers should overtax merchants or, as occasionally happened, unjustly seize their property, merchants would be quick to liquidate their resources and evacuate. Rulers were generally reluctant to engage in such short-sighted practices. Not only did they recognize the important roles that caravan traders served, but they also understood that disaffected merchant groups would have both the motivation and the financial resources to support rival claimants to the throne. In general, early modern rulers took a serious interest in supporting merchants by maintaining a healthy commercial infrastructure.

State investment in trade routes was one of the most visible manifestations of this policy, and in this regard Babur's Mughal heirs fully embraced the supportive policies employed by their Turko-Afghan predecessors. While the Ghaznavid period of rule in India (998–1186) is commonly viewed as one of iconoclastic, disruptive invasions and extractive fiscal policies, the Ghurid, Khilji, Tughluqid and other Turko-Afghan rulers in Delhi generally maintained a concerted effort to enhance the safety of the caravan routes, both by suppressing predatory tribal groups and introducing policies designed to enhance the safety of travellers. Our sources reveal that the Delhi Sultans also worked to extend trade routes and develop new ones, plant trees alongside roads to provide shade for travellers, construct caravanserais to provide shelter and protection for travellers, build fortresses to serve as military outposts in troubled regions, dig wells, and deploy military forces to provide security for travellers.

The successes that the Delhi Sultans enjoyed in these ventures had several important ramifications: they facilitated long-distance trade between India and Central Asia, which strengthened the economies of both regions; they increased urbanization in the Punjab, Multan and Sind; and they led to the development of a highly mercantile culture in the region which was visible in the rising prominence of the Multani merchant families, discussed below, as well as in the development of the commerce-oriented Sikh faith. Rulers leveraged the resources of their states to facilitate caravan traffic, but they were not alone in their efforts. As this commercial culture developed, merchants themselves had a strong interest in investing in the commercial infrastructure, and they likewise financed such projects as digging wells and constructing caravanserais and bridges.

Babur's statement at the beginning of this chapter suggests that Kabul enjoyed an active commercial climate at the beginning of the sixteenth century, which his Mughal heirs worked to maintain. Indeed, trade-friendly policies remained in place even during the temporary expulsion of Babur's son, Humayun (r. 1530–40, 1555–56), from India. To facilitate travel to the north-west, the Afghan ruler Sher Shah Suri (r. 1540–45) financed the construction of the Rohtas Fort near the Salt Range to help pacify the Ghakkars (Gakhars), a tribe loyal to Humayun that had been struggling for dominance in the area and disrupting the trade routes leading to the Khyber Pass and beyond. The chronicler Abbas Khan Sarwani reports that Sher Shah paid for the creation of many thousands of miles of tree-lined roads across northern India. Sher Shah fostered commerce along these roads by ordering the construction of some 1700 caravanserais at regular intervals, each of which was built with facilities to service both Hindu and Muslim travellers.

To ensure the safety of trans-regional trade across his territory, Sher Shah required his *muqaddam*s, the official revenue officers in each village, to be held personally responsible for any unrecovered merchandise stolen in their districts. His policy regarding the murder of a caravan trader was even more rigid. According to Sarwani, if a merchant were killed while travelling in his realm, Sher Shah would hold the *muqaddam*s responsible:

> If they produced the assassins or showed the place of their residence, the muqaddams were set free and the murderers were killed. But if the muqaddams of a village in the jurisdiction of which a murder was committed failed to do this, they were put to death.[2]

From the beginning of Akbar's long reign (r. 1556–1605), the construction of new trade routes and the maintenance of established ones became a defining feature of Mughal economic policy. Akbar's vizier, Abu'l Fazl, recorded in his extraordinarily detailed fiscal report of the Mughal Empire, the *Ain-i Akbari*, that during the latter part of the sixteenth century there were five distinct routes leading from India to Kabul, and caravan traders who wished to make their way from Kabul onwards to Central Asia had no fewer than seven routes to choose from.[3] The most direct route led through the Khyber Pass, and it rapidly became the favoured one after Akbar had the roads improved so that merchants could transport their merchandise using wheeled vehicles as well as pack animals.

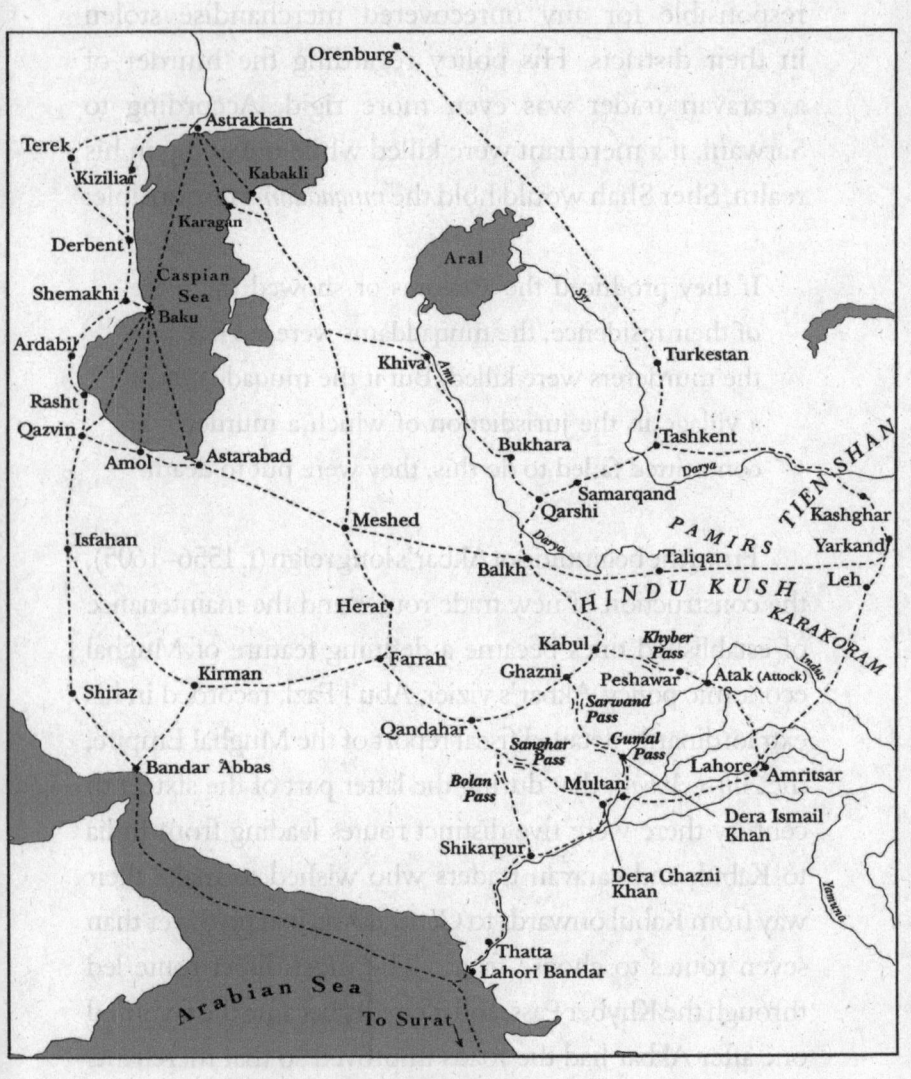

Map of the Principal Trade Routes

(Not to scale)

Of course it was not sufficient only to build the roads. Akbar also needed to ensure the safety of those who would travel along them, and records of his efforts to do so date to very early in his reign. Just two years after he ascended the Mughal throne, the young emperor, who was only sixteen at the time, ordered the Mughal armies to occupy Multan and Lahore and begin the construction of a series of fortresses in the region. Larger fortresses were established at strategic locations such as the one at Atak (Attock), near where the Grand Trunk Road crosses the Indus River, while a network of smaller forts, called *thana*s, extended Mughal authority along the roads that led across the north-west frontier.

The individual who initially spearheaded this initiative was the young emperor's regent, Bairam Khan. Akbar learned well from his mentor and in future years he continued to embrace trade-friendly policies designed to protect and enhance India's overland trade with both Central Asia and Iran. Abu'l Fazl notes that Akbar had many caravanserais built and maintained, for example, and in 1588 he financed the construction of a bridge over the Indus at Atak.[4]

At the same time, Akbar did not hesitate to resort to violence, if it would help maintain peace and safety on the trade routes. For example, after learning that Afghan and Baloch tribes were harassing caravan merchants en route to Qandahar, Akbar ordered his military to intercede. Mughal forces killed thousands of tribesmen, and thousands more were enslaved and removed from their homelands to be sold in foreign markets. In such situations, Akbar was employing the proverbial stick—demonstrating the Mughal military strength and unleashing a terribly punitive measure broadcast for all to see what the Mughals were willing and able to do in order to secure the safety of caravan traders. This policy was a deterrent against parasitic elements bent upon disrupting the caravan trade for their own short-term gains. At the same time, Akbar and his heirs were quite willing to offer the proverbial carrot. This included presenting tribal leaders with generous gifts and other incentives, such as lucrative posts in the Mughal administration.

In short, overland trade with Central Asia was far too important to the empire's economy to leave to chance. In addition to employing bands of *rahdar*s charged with policing the roads, the Mughals maintained Sher Shah's policy of requiring local administrators to compensate caravan traders for any merchandise stolen in their territory. The Mughals are also known to have taken clan leaders and their family members hostage, retaining them at the capital where they served as leverage to ensure that their tribesmen would permit caravan traffic to pass through their territory unmolested.

These policies may seem extreme, but they were comparable to the policies enforced in neighbouring

Safavid Iran and the Bukharan Khanate. Even during times of political conflict among the Mughal, Safavid and Uzbek states, rulers continued to share information on the security of the trade routes and, with only a few (albeit quite notable) exceptions, merchants could count on the support of the rulers. Despite their recurrent conflicts over Qandahar, Akbar and Shah 'Abbas collaborated on a number of initiatives, including bridge and caravanserai construction projects that aimed to improve overland trade between their realms. According to the great Persian ruler's chronicler, Eskandar Beg, Shah 'Abbas believed that 'the greater part of governing is the preservation of stability within the kingdom and security on the roads'.[5]

After security, the establishment and maintenance of a functional system of caravanserais were arguably the most important features in promoting trans-regional trade between India, Central Asia and Iran. While caravanserais were constructed in a great variety of sizes and configurations, they all served functions that were critical to the maintenance of an active trans-regional caravan trade. In rural settings along the trade routes, these included: providing a safe and secure location for weary travellers to rest and find food and water for themselves and their pack animals; functioning as commercial markets where traders from multiple locations could meet and exchange merchandise; and

serving as outposts for state administrators responsible
for supervising commercial interactions and collecting
an entrance fee, a daily fee, taxes and other duties. In
urban settings, caravanserais also functioned as long-
term lodging for international traders. It was not
uncommon for traders to occupy these urban merchant
hostels for years at a time while they engaged in a variety
of commercial activities far from their homeland.

In Central Asia, the Uzbek-Shibanid (1500–99)
rulers of the Bukharan Khanate also placed a great value
on the services that caravan traders provided. In some
ways, it could be argued that, like the Mughals in India,
the Shibanids inherited the policies of their Timurid
predecessors. In any event, it is clear that the Bukharan
Khans found great value in their geographical location
at the centre of Asia, and they worked to promote
commercial traffic with their neighbours in India, and
elsewhere, throughout the early modern era.[6]

The Shibanid ruler Abdullah Khan II (r. 1583–98)
was especially proactive in this regard. In 1557, even
before he replaced his father, Iskandar (r. 1561–83), on the
throne, Abdullah occupied his future capital of Bukhara
and began a series of initiatives designed to enhance the
city's international trade. This included financing the
construction of caravanserais, covered markets and other
commercial institutions in cities across the Khanate.

Within the city of Bukhara itself, Abdullah financed the construction of several new covered markets: one for hat sellers (*taq-i tilpaq furushan*), one for goldsmiths (*taq-i zargaran*) and another for money changers and bankers (*taq-i sarrafan*). Even today the *taq-i sarrafan* remains a monument in the heart of Bukhara's old city, located adjacent to an open park that was previously the location of one of several Indian caravanserais in the city.

Bukharan Caravanserai (1890s)

Abdullah sent his first ambassador to the court of Emperor Akbar in 1572, and the two exchanged a series of embassies until Abdullah's death in 1598. Abdullah's diplomatic exchanges with Akbar had several objectives, not the least of which was to convince Akbar to join forces and wage war against the Shia Muslim Safavids, after which, he proposed, they could divide Persia between them. Akbar politely, but sternly, refused to support this proposition. It is striking that, throughout their diplomatic correspondence, both rulers repeatedly assert their commitment to do everything within their power to maintain the security of the roads, encourage the caravan trade and assist traders from each other's realm in their own territory.

Following the fall of the Shibanid dynasty, the similarly Uzbek Ashtarkhanid (also known as the Janid, or Toqay-Timurid) dynasty (1599–1747) remained dedicated to fostering a climate conducive to trans-regional trade. This is also evidenced in diplomatic correspondence, in which both sides repeatedly reaffirm their desire to work together to keep the roads safe for caravan traders travelling between their realms. In one such letter, a copy of which is included in a manuscript collection of the Ashtarkhanid rulers' official correspondence, a Bukharan Khan addresses Nawab Fathallah Khan, the Mughal *hakim* (governor) of Kabul, and requests that he 'please help (the merchant) Mehter Hamdam to quickly purchase textiles and other things and take them back to Bukhara'.[7] For their part, the Bukharans are known to have offered assistance to caravan traders from other regions who passed through

Bukhara on their way to India. For instance, in another letter in the same collection, the Ashtarkhanid ruler Subhan Quli Khan (r. 1681–1702) notifies an Iraqi noble:

> We have sent your humble servant to India for the purchase of textiles and goods for you, the axis of the universe. We have now heard that this person has completed his duties in the traditional manner and has returned to Kabul, the threshold of the universe.[8]

Considering the relationship between caravan traders and the state throughout the early modern era, one finds relatively few examples of short-sighted, predatory states willing to ruin fortunes, and their reputations, for short-term gain. That said, sometimes rulers failed to provide the security that the merchants needed, and governmental policies were known to change over time, sometimes for the better and sometimes not. For example, shortly after Jahangir (r. 1605–27) ascended the throne after the death of his aged father, Akbar, he sought to draw more caravans from Central Asia and Iran. Jahangir slashed taxes, expanded caravanserai construction, and issued a number of edicts to protect merchants. These policies were then reversed under Jahangir's son,

Shah Jahan (r. 1628–58), who not only reinstated the old taxes but also added new ones. In 1646–47, Shah Jahan further disrupted Mughal relations with Bukhara by unleashing a massive, and ill-fated, invasion of Balkh. The disruption was temporary, however. Shortly after Shah Jahan's son Aurangzeb (r. 1658–1707) wrested the throne from his father, the Bukharan Khan 'Abd al-Aziz (r. 1645–81) dispatched an ambassador to the Mughal court. The Bukharan ambassador delivered a letter to his former adversary that called for 'love and friendship between us'.[9] The letter includes the following appeal:

> Before this period, in the time of the great ones, there was a steady relationship which had become our tradition. We would like the same relations to be protected and continued in this time. The sending of messengers and goods on both sides should be the practice.[10]

Aurangzeb's subsequent efforts at reasserting Mughal authority in Kabul and maintaining the security of the trade routes to the north and west indicate that he agreed with his Bukharan neighbour.

One benefit of the mutual emphasis on protecting the caravan trade was that traffic moved sufficiently fast for the Mughals to receive the legendary fruit of

Central Asia—which Babur had famously longed for in the wake of his expulsion from Samarqand—while it was still fresh. Indeed, as a way to entice Aurangzeb to renew their friendly relations, 'Abd al-Aziz Khan's embassy included, as a gift, two hundred camels loaded with fruit: one hundred carrying fresh fruit, and another hundred carrying dried. In subsequent years, fresh fruit from Central Asia could be found in markets even as far as the Deccan. Writing in the latter half of the seventeenth century, the French traveller François Bernier observed that

Hindoustan consumes an immense quantity of fresh fruit from Samarkand, Bali [Balkh], Bocara, and Persia; such as melons, apples pears and grapes, eaten at Dehli and purchased at a very high price nearly the whole winter—and likewise dried fruit, such as almonds, pistachio and various other small nuts, plums, apricots, and raisins, which may be procured the whole year round . . . [In Delhi,] there is, indeed, a fruit-market that makes some show. It contains many shops which during the summer are well supplied with dry fruit from Persia, Balk, Bokara, and Samarkande; such as almonds, pistachios, and walnuts, raisins, prunes, and apricots; and in winter with excellent fresh grapes, black and white, brought from the same countries, wrapped in cotton; pears and apples of three or four sorts, and those admirable melons which last the whole winter. These fruites are, however, very dear; a single melon selling for a crown and a half. But nothing is considered so great a treat: it forms the chief expense of the Omrahs, and I have frequently known my Agah spend twenty crowns on fruit for his breakfast.[11]

This was, of course, a shrewd calculation on the part of the Uzbek Khan. 'Abd al-Aziz was keenly aware that the Mughal nobility included many migrants from Central Asia, who retained a similar appreciation for the fabled fruit of their homeland. Even though they were no longer in his service, 'Abd al-Aziz was no doubt eager to use their influence at the Mughal court to his advantage.

3. MULTANIS AND SHIKARPURIS

The Multanis and Sahs [moneylenders] of Delhi who have
acquired abundant wealth have derived it from the resources
(daulat) of the old nobles (maliks and amirs) of Delhi.
The latter took loans from the Multanis and Sahs beyond
limit, and repaid the advances with largesses (by drafts)
upon their iqtas (revenue assignments). The moment a
khan or malik held an assembly and invited notables as
guests, his functionaries rushed to the Multanis and Sahs,
and giving them drafts (qabz'ha) upon themselves took
loans at interest.[1]

—Barani, referring to events during the
reign of the slave-king Balban (r. 1266–87)

As the previous chapter suggests, the caravan trade
connecting Indian markets with those in Central

Asia remained vibrant throughout the early modern era. The majority of the merchants involved in this trade were commonly referred to as Multanis because of their association with wealthy family firms based in that city. In addition to their investments within India, the Multani firms were exceptionally successful in trans-regional trade with markets to the north and west. As one might expect, this success attracted young apprentices eager to make their own fortunes. The present chapter investigates the rise of the Multanis in the South Asian context, tracing their history to the thirteenth century, when they first appear in historical sources. We will identify a number of factors that contributed to the Multanis' development under the Delhi Sultans and their Mughal successors.

By the middle of the sixteenth century, increased competition within India motivated the Multanis to expand their business interests geographically, by dispatching agents to take up residence in markets beyond the boundaries of the subcontinent where they could take advantage of similar commercial opportunities in less competitive settings. The Multani firms maintained expansive and diverse commercial portfolios in both trade and moneylending, and their agents exhibited remarkable skill and fortitude in negotiating these new markets. Subsequent chapters will address the Multanis' operations in Central Asia and other Eurasian regions, and the various factors that brought about an end to their trade in those places. But first, we must understand how the foundations of that trade developed within the subcontinent.

The Multanis

Indian caravan traders are known to have visited Central Asian markets in antiquity, although it is only in the early modern era that we find evidence of an Indian merchant diaspora spread across the region. This was an expansive network of semi-permanent communities inhabited by a circulating population of trained agents who remained stationed abroad for any number of years before eventually returning home. Arguably the earliest report of Indians in Central Asia operating in a manner consistent with diaspora commerce can be attributed to an Englishman, Anthony Jenkinson. In 1558, Jenkinson visited Bukhara in his capacity as an agent of the ill-fated Muscovy Company, a joint stock company charged with exploring the possibility of establishing an overland route to the Indian Ocean through Russia. During his three-month stay in Bukhara, Jenkinson encountered a community of Indian merchants who reportedly spent years at a time living in the region.[2]

At roughly the same time as Jenkinson made his observations, two other Central Asian sources provide some insight into the composition of these Indian communities. Legal records dating to 1559 and 1561 identify 'Multanis' as having settled and owned property in Bukhara.[3] In 1584, the official chronicler of the Uzbek ruler Abdullah Khan lamented that a group of merchants from Multan were among those caravan traders who lost their merchandise due to a warehouse fire in Peshawar.[4] Just a short time later, from 1589–90, a *qadi* in Samarqand made eight entries in his legal record that refer to a number of Multanis by name, and describe some of their commercial activities.[5] Other sixteenth-century sources refer to Indian caravanserais in both Tashkent and Bukhara, and later sources provide a rich portrait of the Indian commercial presence in Central Asia.

The numbers of Multanis occupying communities in Central Asia, and other Eurasian locations, grew rapidly in the seventeenth century. In 1623, F.A. Kotov, a Russian merchant, encountered a Multani community in the Safavid capital of Isfahan. Over several decades the Multanis developed an exceptionally large commercial presence in Iran, with several observers estimating that the capital alone was home to 10,000 Multanis or more. In the 1660s, the French traveller Jean Chardin suggested that the number of 'Multani Indians' in all of the Safavid territories exceeded 20,000.[6] Though the number of Multanis in Central Asia was smaller than in Iran, there too they represented the major part of the Indian commercial presence. One Central Asian chronicle compiled in the early eighteenth century, the *Tadhkira-i Muqim Khani*, presents an anecdote pertaining to the Bukharan ruler Imam Quli Khan (r. 1611–41) in which the author specifically refers to an entire 'Indian quarter' of the city which was almost certainly populated primarily by Multanis.[7]

The excerpt that begins this chapter, taken from Zia al-Din Barani's fourteenth-century *Tarikh-i-Firuz Shahi*, demonstrates that Multanis had been active in India long before they became commercial fixtures in Central Asia, Persia and other Eurasian locations. We note that Barani takes care to distinguish them from other moneylenders (*sahs*) and, looking back to the thirteenth century, he identifies them as wealthy creditors, for interest, to the nobility of the Delhi Sultanate. But who were these Multanis?

Most obviously, Multanis were natives of Multan, which in the premodern period was both a region in north-western India wedged between Sind and the

Punjab, and an ancient city that was the capital of that region. The city of Multan was recognized as an important outpost for the caravan trade to the north-west even before Alexander the Great was injured taking the city in 326 BCE. In antiquity, the city was referred to as Mulastana or Mulastanapura. It only became known as Multan following the eighth-century Umayyad conquest of the region. As a regional capital, medieval Multan drew great luminaries from throughout India to the east, and the Islamic world to the west.

Geographically, Multan was situated in a fertile stretch near the confluence of the Ravi and the Chenab, which provided water for agricultural settlements as well as waterways leading southwards to the Indian Ocean. At the same time, Multan offered easy access to the overland caravan routes that connected India with its neighbours to the north and west, via the Khyber Pass, and on to Kabul; the Gumal Pass, and on to Ghazni; and the Bolan and Sanghar passes, which both lead to Qandahar. In the tenth and eleventh centuries, medieval Arab geographers found that Multan continued to serve as a major commercial centre mediating India's trade with the Islamic world. By the thirteenth century, the Indian merchant communities that dedicated themselves to mediating that trade were known in India and elsewhere as Multanis.

The significance of both Multan and the Multanis grew dramatically during the period of Delhi Sultanate rule in the region (1206–1555). In the early fourteenth century, Zia al-Din Barani identified Multanis as trans-regional commercial agents for the Delhi Sultanate nobility. In this capacity, Barani mentioned the Multanis alongside *sudagar*s (traders), although he took care to distinguish between the two. As mentioned above, he also referred to them alongside *sah*s (moneylenders) as creditors to the nobility, while distinguishing between these groups as well. The only explanation for this distinction is that, while the Multanis were engaged in the same types of trade and moneylending ventures as *sudagar*s and *sah*s, and their interests are certain to have overlapped, the Multanis' interest in trans-regional trade was a defining feature of their commercial activities, while the same was not true for *sudagar*s and *sah*s.

Throughout the early modern era, Indian textile exports represented an especially important part of the Multanis' trade, and this too seems to have its origins in earlier centuries. Barani mentions, for example, that at one point during his reign 'Ala' al-Din Khalji (r. 1296–1316) grew concerned with the rising prices of ordinary textiles, an absolute necessity for the population at large. In an effort to address this problem, he issued a *farman* that required 'Multanis and *sudagar*s' to sell common textiles at a *sultani*, fixed, rate. He then promoted this trade by subsidizing it with some two million tanga, which he had his treasury advance to wealthy Multanis.[8] Considering their trans-regional interests, we can conclude that, already during the thirteenth and fourteenth centuries, Multanis were heavily involved in the export trade of Indian textiles and other goods to markets in Central Asia and Iran.

An Integrated Commercial System

Already by the thirteenth century, Multani firms controlled a substantial amount of capital, which they used to finance a variety of commercial ventures in multiple markets throughout north India. To put it in other terms, one might categorize the Multanis of Barani's account as proto-portfolio capitalists, precursors to the Jagat Seth 'World Banker' banking house and the other great merchant houses of the seventeenth and eighteenth centuries.[9] We will soon turn our attention to the Multanis who began to appear in historical records in Central Asia during the second half of the sixteenth century. But to gain an improved understanding of the types of commercial activities they were engaged in there, we will first look back in time to determine their activities in India.

The Multanis exhibited a number of similarities with *sudagar*s (or *tujjar*, traders) and *sah*s (or *sahu*, also *shah*, moneylenders). But the Multanis' engagement in multiple types of commercial activities makes it impossible to categorize them simply as either merchants or bankers. In practice, Multani firms engaged in a wide variety of overlapping commercial interests, which they fully exploited to great advantage. For example, while some sources focus on the Multanis' trade activities, other historical sources refer to Multanis as *sarraf*s, or *shroff*s, money changers who were sufficiently skilled in numismatic metallurgy to assess the value of the many gold, silver and other coins in circulation and to exchange them, for a profit, while also providing a variety of other financial services. In the seventeenth century, the French jeweller Tavernier observed:

In India a village must be very small indeed if it has not a money-changer, called a Shroff, who acts as banker to make remittances of money and issue letters of exchange [hundis] . . . All the Jews who occupy themselves with money and exchange in the empire of the Grand Seigneur [the Ottoman Sultan] pass for being very sharp; but in India they would scarcely be apprentices to these Changers.[10]

A term closely related to *sarraf* is the seth, which identifies a wealthy moneylender who could provide a number of services necessary to conduct large-scale trade. Most famous among these is the Marwari Jagat Seth banking house, founded in the middle of the seventeenth century by Hiranand Sahu and brought to prosperity in the eighteenth century under the direction of his son, Seth Manik Chand.[11] Both *sarraf*s and seths are commonly referred to in European sources simply as bankers, and like the Marwari Jagat Seths, the Multani *sarraf*s were also organized around the principle of the Indian family firm.

The family firm model was a critical component of the Indians' success for several reasons, not the least of which was that it enabled agents of established firms to utilize the financial technologies of the time to minimize risk as they moved large amounts of wealth across great distances. The *hundi* was doubtless the most important of these technologies. For caravan traders and others involved in commercial ventures, travelling with large amounts of cash posed certain obvious security risks. *Hundi*s were an excellent solution to that problem. Commonly defined as a 'bill of exchange', a *hundi* was a document drawn up in highly formulaic language that promised payment of a specified amount by a particular firm upon the presentation of the document.

For example, an individual travelling from Multan to Golconda for the purchase of precious stones could hand over a large sum of cash or merchandise to a *sarraf* (or *seth*) in Multan in exchange for a *hundi* that stipulated a certain value. Upon the merchant's arrival in Golconda, the merchant would present that *hundi* to an agent affiliated with the same family firm, who would encash it according to the instructions included in the document, minus a small fee.

*Hundi*s were fully saleable instruments, meaning firms could buy and sell them, and use them as a negotiable medium for transmitting large amounts of wealth among multiple financial houses across great distances. They were also fully secure, meaning that were it lost or stolen, the holder did not suffer a financial loss. Rather, the agent who issued it could confirm the existence of the *hundi* and its value, and the holder would eventually be paid in full. For all these reasons, *hundi*s were widely used for commercial payments and other transfers of capital within India, and they were absolutely critical for the commercial success of Indian family firms in Central Asia.

An example that illustrates the utility of the *hundi* in this regard can be found in the account of the British agent Alexander Burnes, who, in the 1830s, was sent on a diplomatic mission to the Amir of Bukhara.

Upon his arrival in Kabul, Burnes located a reputable banker and encashed a *hundi* that he already had in his possession for 5000 rupees. The same 'banker' then offered to issue Burnes an additional *hundi* that he could take with him and encash with the banker's associates in Nizhny Novgorod, Astrakhan or Bukhara. Burnes eagerly accepted the latter, exclaiming, 'How much is our wonder excited to find the ramifications of commerce extending uninterruptedly over such vast and remote regions, differing as they do from each other in language, religion, manners, and law'.[12] He would have been no less astonished had he made his journey in the sixteenth century.

Two other categories of merchants are relevant to our discussion of the Multani firms in India: the *dallal* and the *baqqal*. The *dallal* was a market broker who purchased large quantities of bulk goods from farmers, such as cotton or grains, and arranged to have them transported to wholesalers in regional markets. The *baqqal* was a wholesaler who dealt specifically in the grain trade. As merchants associated with the Multanis and other banking houses, these brokers and wholesalers were known to provide loans to farmers in the form of commercial credit and materials, such as seeds and livestock, in exchange for a percentage of the finished crop. They were also known to purchase the remainder of the crop and arrange for its transport to wholesale markets, thereby monetizing the rural economy and facilitating the collection of taxes in cash. The Delhi Sultans and other rulers in India found this to be an exceptionally valuable service, and it earned the merchants the support of the state.

Wherever they were established, the Multani firms exhibited an impressive degree of diversification in their economic interests. While some specific Multani firms may have specialized in the cotton trade and others in grain, as a whole, Multani firms enlisted large numbers of *gumashta*s, or agents, who simultaneously engaged in a variety of commercial ventures. Already in the fourteenth century, Barani noted that Multanis were heavily invested in the textile trade while also serving as large-scale creditors for the Delhi Sultanate nobility. Five centuries later, Mountstuart Elphinstone observed that agents of Indian firms in Afghanistan continued to 'mix trade and agency with their regular banking business' in order to exploit every opportunity available to them.

The Multani network in north India was a highly integrated commercial system that exploited every available opportunity for profit. This was also the case for those Multanis who spent years at a time conducting business in Central Asia and other distant

Eurasian locations. Thus, while some Multanis worked outside of India as traders (*sudagar*s, *tujjar*) engaged in the exportation of Indian cottons to foreign markets, other sources identify them principally as shrewd merchant-moneylenders (seths/*sahs* or *sarrafs*). Still other sources identify Multani agents both within India and elsewhere at the village level (*baqqal*), where they extended credit to farmers in exchange for a part of the harvest. The moneylender would then arrange for the finished product to be transferred to another creditor who functioned as a commodity broker (*dallal*), and distributed the agricultural production to wholesale markets (*mandi*s). As diversified as this system was, it should be stressed that it did not operate in isolation, or without competition.[13]

Under the Delhi Sultans, the Multanis appear to have enjoyed considerable success at extending their network throughout northern India, and they became even more prosperous under the Mughals. Quite early during Akbar's reign, in the middle of the sixteenth century, the Multani family firms are known to have sent their agents to the less competitive markets beyond the subcontinent. These markets offered tempting opportunities for the family firm directors and, while some Multani agents consolidated their firm's position in India, tens of thousands more ventured beyond the Hindu Kush to pursue similar interests in foreign markets, establishing a trade network that covered virtually all of southern Central Asia, Afghanistan and Persia, and reached up the Caucasus and far into Russia. Before we direct our attention to the commercial activities of these Indians abroad, one final question remains: Just who were the Multanis?

The Multani Identity

The designation 'Multani' identifies Indian merchants whose communities were centred in that region and were heavily engaged in trade and other commercial activities that linked India with regions far beyond the north-western frontiers of the subcontinent. But beyond that, the term says nothing about the Indian communities to which they belonged. Digging into our sources, we find that the Multanis were a surprisingly broad-based and diverse patchwork of caste identities and multiple religious traditions.

The vast majority of Multanis who took up residence in Central Asia can be identified with the Hindu religious tradition. But from the beginning, the designation 'Multani' referred to both Hindu and Muslim merchants belonging to multiple 'caste' identities. To cite an early example: according to

Barani, in the thirteenth century, the Delhi Sultan 'Ala' al-Din Khalji's chief *qadi*, a man named Hamid al-Din, was the son of a Multani moneylender.[14] In Central Asia as well, the earliest available records that mention Multanis refer to a number of Muslim Multanis, some of whom had commercial interactions with Hindu Multanis. In Bukharan legal records dating to 1559 and 1561, two Indian landowners are identified as Maulana Omar Multani ibn Maulana Abd al-Wahab Multani and Baba Multani ibn Ali.[15] Later in the sixteenth century, a register belonging to a Samarqandi *qadi* includes a number of documents that pertain to the commercial activities of several Muslim Multanis. The most important of these individuals was Janab Darya Khan Multani ibn Janab Sheikh Sa'adi Multani, who appears in eight entries as a major creditor to the Multani community and was heavily involved in the textile trade. The following is a translation of one of these entries:

This thirteenth day of the month of Muharram al-Haram, in the year 999 (11 November 1590), Ustad Gujar Multani, son of Khwaja Ya'qub, being of full legal competence, made the following statement, true and in accordance with the law: 'I must give and deliver to the aforementioned beneficiary (Darya

Khan Multani, son of Sheikh Sa'di), thirty-two pieces of red chit-i purband, each twelve gaz long and one mukassar gaz wide. This I will deliver to the person mentioned above, who is the beneficiary of this statement, in the city of Samarqand, in seven full months'.[16]

In addition to several apparently non-Muslim Indians (e.g., Lahori Chitgar ibn Lalu), other entries in the same judicial record refer to Muslim Multanis, such as Ustad Rajab Kazar Multani ibn Ustan Hussain Multani, Mankui Kazar Multani, Mullah Hussain ibn Paina Multani, Allahdad ibn Jahan Shah Multani and Khwaja Ibrahim Multani ibn Abdallah Multani.[17] In the seventeenth century, several of the more astute European travellers to Safavid Iran also observed that a portion of the roughly 20,000 Multanis who lived there were Muslims.

It is likely that at least some of the Muslim Multanis were in fact Lohani, or some other community of Afghan Powindas known to have operated a pastoral network that stretched from Bukhara and its environs in the north, even as far as the Deccan and Bengal. These Afghan Powinda pastoralists, or *kuchis*, are known to have been deeply involved in India's trade with Central Asia. Every spring, extended Powinda families led their *qafila*s (caravans) of thousands of camels loaded with Indian good across Afghanistan to Central Asian markets, returning southwards in the fall with tens of thousands of Central Asian horses. It is likely that many of the 10,000– 20,000 Indian merchants ('heads-of-houses') that Babur says made their way up to Kabul each year were Lohani Powindas. This was nothing new to the region, but it seems quite likely that, in the later sixteenth century, as Emperor Akbar and Abdullah Khan II normalized diplomatic relations and mutually encouraged the movement of traders and goods between their states, the Lohani and other Powinda groups would have been among the first communities to take advantage of the improved situation.

As pastoralists, Powinda tribesmen moved freely between these regions on an annual basis. This further enhanced the vitality of India's trade with Central Asia, as Powinda clans moving back and forth between India and Central Asia were in a unique position to contract with Multani firms to move large quantities of merchandise, information, *hundi*s and Multani agents themselves safely across the Hindu Kush. At the same time, other Powindas, such as Darya Khan, appear to have set aside the pastoral way of life and capitalized on their successes by launching their own Multani firms.

These dynamics appear to have been in place throughout the early modern era. In 1751, a Tatar traveller from Astrakhan to Khiva, Bukhara and Balkh found Afghan Powindas actively transporting bulk goods to these areas from as far away as Calcutta.[18] In the nineteenth century, Alexander Burnes's exceptionally astute Kashmiri companion, Mohan Lal, reported that Lohani and Shikarpuri merchants continued to dominate the movement of goods between Bukhara and Multan, also noting that many of them continued onwards into India reaching even Calcutta, Bombay and beyond.

The Lohani and other Powinda tribesmen mediated much of the caravan trade, primarily by orchestrating the logistics involved in moving thousands of tons of merchandise across mountains and deserts and also, it seems, in giving rise to their own Multani firms. But it is clear that neither the Lohanis, nor any other Muslim group, represented the major part of the Multani population. The vast majority of the Multani merchants who ventured to Central Asia, Persia and other distant markets adhered to other non-Muslim Indian religious traditions.

Several contemporary sources refer to the Multanis as Banians (or Banias), implying that they belonged to a commercial caste associated with the Hindu or Jain religious traditions. Tavernier's observation, dating to 1676, is typical:

> Multan is the place from whence all the Banians migrate who come to trade in Persia, where they follow the same occupation as the Jews . . . and they surpass them in their usury.[19]

A few years earlier, Thévenot similarly observed that, although Multan was ruled by Muslims,

> it contains a great many Banians also, for Multan is their chief rendezvous for trading into Persia, where they do what the Jews do in other places; but they are far more cunning, for nothing escapes them, and they let slip no occasion of getting the penny, how small soever it be.[20]

Thévenot was careful to distinguish Banians from Khatris, another merchant group that was present in Multan in large numbers and that was heavily invested in trans-regional trade with Afghanistan and Central Asia.

It is difficult to trace the history of the Khatri community with any great accuracy. It seems reasonably well established, however, that the Khatri presence in the Punjab and the surrounding areas long predates the earliest Ghaznavid incursions into the region. It is interesting to note that, unlike the Banians, who are associated with the third of the Hindu classes, the Vaisya (mercantile) *varna*, the Khatris are generally recognized to be Kshatriyas, or members of the second (warrior) *varna*, following only the Brahmins.

It is quite well established that Khatris maintained close relations with the Mughal nobility, and they prospered in early modern India largely due to Mughal patronage.[21] We saw in the previous chapter that rulers in both Mughal India and Uzbek Central Asia maintained policies designed to encourage trade between the two regions. Because of their communal predisposition for trade and their concentration in the Punjab, Multan and Sind, the Khatris stood to benefit greatly from such efforts. Indeed, evidence suggests that the Khatris even partnered with rulers, which highlights Mughal motivations to support their commercial ventures both within India and in foreign markets.[22] This support was likely to have been critical to the early establishment of Indian merchant communities in Central Asia during the sixteenth and seventeenth centuries. But that is not to say that the fate of the merchants was bound inextricably to their political patrons. We will see that these communities persisted long after the decline of Mughal imperial authority in India, and they survived several dynastic shifts in Central Asia as well.

Thévenot observed that the Khatris maintained a vast commercial network that emanated from Multan to 'spread all over the Indies'.[23] In the nineteenth century, Mountstuart Elphinstone and George Campbell visited Afghanistan a few years apart and independently identified the majority of the Indian merchant community there as Khatris. In the 1830s, Elphinstone found the Khatris to be present throughout Afghanistan, and as far afield as Astrakhan, in Russia.[24] Campbell found that these exceptionally skilful merchants were so entrenched in the Afghan commercial economy that 'no village can get on without the Khatri who keeps the accounts, does the banking business, and buys and sells the grain'. He further expressed his amazement at their commercial success both within India and beyond its boundaries, declaring:

> I do not know the exact limits of Khatri occupation to the West, but certainly in all Eastern Afghanistan they seem to be just as much a part of the established community as they are in the Punjab. They find their way far into Central Asia.[25]

This network was no less extensive in the early twentieth century, when the Indian economic historian L.C. Jain wrote that Khatris (identified more precisely as Aroras, a subcategory of the Khatris) continued to 'control the finance of much of the commerce of India with central Asia, Afghanistan and Tibet'.[26]

Later records from the Russian colonial period and from the archives of the Office of the Bukharan Khushbegi (vizier) indicate that a great many of the so-called Banians living in the region could be more precisely identified as Bhatias, a merchant community that had been established in and around Sind since antiquity. Like the Khatris, the Bhatias had a long history in the Multani region, and in the early modern era they were also known to have established a satellite community in Dera Ismail Khan, a frontier town near the Gumal Pass that served as a winter headquarters for certain groups of Powinda nomads. Additional evidence points to individuals who can be identified as Khojas, Bohras and other merchant castes who similarly participated in India's trade with Central Asia.

Marwari Jains represent another, albeit smaller, contingent of Indian merchants active in early modern Central Asia, Russia and other markets beyond the boundaries of the subcontinent. Shortly after the Jain Oswals gave rise to the Jagat Seth banking house in Marwar in the seventeenth century, Jain family firms began to follow in the footsteps of the Multanis by dispatching agents to distant markets. The earliest records of Marwaris in Astrakhan date to the seventeenth century, while other archival records demonstrate that Marwaris remained active in Central Asia even into the 1880s. In both Russia and Central Asia, the senior figures of these communities were identified independently, and 150 years apart, by the same title: Marwari Baraev, or 'The Great Marwari'.

During the nineteenth century, and possibly before, adherents to the Sikh faith, centred in Amritsar, also began to appear in Central Asia alongside Hindus, Muslims and Jains. The fact that our sources document the presence of a small and quite prosperous Sikh community in Central Asia should not come as a surprise, considering that many Sikhs had ancestral roots in the Khatri community. The Sikhs who made their way to Central Asia in the nineteenth century were likely to have been descendants of Multani Khatris who elected to follow the Sikh Panth and relocate to Amritsar. Indeed, during the eighteenth century, a number of factors led a significant portion of the Multani firms to abandon Multan for other locations in the region, including Amritsar although primarily Shikarpur. This topic will be discussed in the next chapter.

4. INDIAN MERCHANTS IN CENTRAL ASIA

The Indians doe bring fine whites, which the Tartars doe roll about their heads, and all other kinds of whites, which serve for apparell made of cotton wooll and crasko [coarse linen], but golde, silver, pretious stones, and spices they bring none . . . The Indians carry from Boghar [Bukhara] again wrought silks, red hides, slaves, and horses, with such like, but of kersies [kersey, an English woolen textile] and other cloth, they make little accompt. I offered to barter with Marchants of those Countreis, which came from the furthest parts of India, even from the Countrey of Bengala, & the River Ganges, to give them kersies for their commodities, but they would not barter for such commoditie as cloth.[1]

—Anthony Jenkinson, Bukhara, 1558

The previous chapter introduced the Multanis from their early history during the Delhi Sultanate period through their rise to prominence in the Mughal era. As we have seen, already during the thirteenth and fourteenth centuries, the Multanis were heavily involved in the textile trade, both within north India and with distant markets beyond the Hindu Kush. This chapter will discuss the specific methods that the Multanis, and other Indian merchant groups, used to extend and maintain a vast commercial network across much of the Eurasian landmass.

The fact that dozens of Indian communities, ranging in size from several individuals to several hundred individuals, were able to thrive in Central Asia for several centuries seems counterintuitive. This is especially so when one considers that the vast majority were Hindus living in rather conservative Muslim states. Indeed, evidence in historical literature suggests that Central Asians generally felt contempt for their Indian neighbours, whom they considered shrewd and exploitative usurers, and whose foreign customs and foreign allegiances most certainly brought them under suspicion.

This chapter will illustrate the Multanis' expansion from India to Central Asia. Despite friction with their neighbours, the Multanis enjoyed a remarkable level of hospitality from the governing administrators who welcomed them into their cities and villages, and protected them with laws and, when necessary, soldiers. Several factors motivated these accommodations, and two of these stand out. First, as trans-regional traders the Indians were able to provide large supplies of cloth and other merchandise from India that enjoyed great demand in Central Asian markets. Second, the moneylending services the Indians provided in both urban and rural markets helped to monetize and strengthen the regional economy. In Central Asia, and wherever else they were found, the Indian merchants used their capital resources as an engine for agricultural production and trans-regional trade.

Devising a Diaspora

In the previous chapter, we outlined the Multanis' impressively diversified commercial network as it spanned the north Indian urban and rural landscape, connecting Indian producers to both domestic and foreign markets. From their homes in Multan, *sahs*, the principals, or firm directors whose capital investments propelled this system, recruited countless *gumashtas*, apprenticed them, and then sent them to work in interrelated markets. Some Multani agents were active in making loans to farmers in exchange for a share of the harvest. Others negotiated the purchase of the harvest and its transportation to regional markets for sale at wholesale rates. Still others arranged with Powindas for the trans-regional transportation of bulk merchandise to distant markets.

In the sixteenth century, a number of factors led the Multanis to expand this system even further by dispatching their most ambitious and adventurous *gumashta*s to distant markets beyond the Hindu Kush. The earliest references place them in Bukhara and Qazvin, the capital cities of the Shibanid and Safavid dynasties at the time. From there, the Indians expanded their activities into Balkh, Samarqand, Tashkent, Qarshi and many other Shibanid cities, as well as Herat and Qandahar, Isfahan, Shiraz, Bandar Abbas, Tabriz, Baku, Astrakhan, and up the Volga as far as Moscow and even St Petersburg. By the middle of the seventeenth century, at any given point in time one could find some 35,000 Indian merchants—the vast majority of whom were Multanis—inhabiting cities and villages in dozens of Eurasian locations.

Several contributing factors led to the development of this remarkable early modern phenomenon. The first was a general increase in Indian market activity during the early modern era, spurred by the commercial activities

Map of the Multani and Shikarpuri Merchant Diaspora

(Not to scale)

of Portuguese merchants who, from the early sixteenth century, began to flood the Indian markets with American silver in exchange for Indian spices and textiles. Within a few decades of Columbus's initial voyage in 1492, the Spanish and Portuguese colonial enterprises had developed a major presence in the Americas, dedicated to seizing the gold and silver in circulation and using forced labour in the rapidly growing mining towns to extract thousands of tons more each year. The figures for the sixteenth century are staggering, and they only increased over time: Spanish mining towns produced more silver in the eighteenth century than they had acquired in the sixteenth and seventeenth centuries combined, for example. As this wealth circulated throughout the globe, it led to dramatic changes in the social, political and, more importantly, economic structures in many locations throughout the early modern world.

Several observers referenced the impacts these developments had in India, where gold and silver deposits in the ground were scarce but agricultural production was abundant. To cite one example, the seventeenth-century French traveller François Bernier summarizes, 'Gold and silver, after circulating in every other quarter of the globe, come at length to be swallowed up, lost in some measure, in *Hindoustan*'.[2] A similar view was expressed by another contemporary traveller, the French monk

Raphaël du Mans, who compared the territory of Safavid Persia to a great caravanserai with two doors, with silver entering through one in the West, only to exit through another in the East where it would pass into India, 'where all the money in the Universe is unloaded as if into an abyss'.[3] From the sixteenth century, with only periodic disruptions, the sustained increase in European demand for Indian agricultural goods spurred production, and this correspondingly created new opportunities for Indian business communities.

Equally important to the Indians' success in Central Asia is that they had amassed substantial capital resources, they had mastered the technical skills required for long-distance commercial transactions, and they had already developed a fully integrated commercial system in north India that encouraged flexibility and expansion. Additionally, because of the caste-based nature of these firms, the Multanis were able to recruit a nearly inexhaustible supply of 'family' as junior agents for the expansion of their firms. Doing so gave the principal investors, the firm directors, extralegal control over the activities of their agents, and access to a variety of recourses to recover the principal investment should one of their agents abscond with the firm's money.

In the first chapter of this volume, we discussed multiple ways in which the Delhi Sultanate and

Mughal administrations worked to build and maintain infrastructures that facilitated trans-regional trade between India and Central Asia. We have also seen that Powinda nomads were well suited to orchestrate the caravan trade between India and Central Asia even in the absence of the state, as they were quite adept at managing their own security needs. But the state's approval was critical for the establishment of Indian communities in Central Asia. Without official permission and protection, it would not have been possible for thousands of Hindu Indian merchants to take up residence in Islamic Central Asia for years at a time.

The official patronage of the Bukharan state therefore represents a third factor critical to the success of Indian merchants in Central Asia. This appears to date to the middle of the sixteenth century, and we can therefore say with some confidence that the earliest Multanis would have had an established presence in Bukhara some time before available documentary evidence places them there in 1559. Their subsequent expansion in the region during the latter half of the sixteenth century was very likely a product of the improved diplomatic relations between the Uzbeks and Mughals during the long reigns of Abdullah Khan (r. 1561/83– 98) and Emperor Akbar (r. 1556–1605). Several decades later, a seventeenth-century Bukharan *farman*, or official mandate, both reaffirmed and formalized the Bukharan position towards their Indian 'guests':

> We are thinking about the condition of the greater community of people. Those of other religions obey the farmans that we make and help us very much. For this reason we will weaken the grip of those who try to oppress them. The goods and property of these people should not become ruined; they are protected. Their protection will come from here and their hopes should be directed to Bukhara. Regarding the Hindus who live in the territories of Bukhara, Balkh, Badakhshan, Qunduz, Taliqan, Aibek, Ghuri, Baghlan, Shabarghan, Termiz, Samarqand, Nasaf (Qarshi), Kish, Shahrisabz, and wherever else they may live: who knows the *aqsaqal* (community elder) must obey and respect him as he is working in their best interest.[4]

Indian Portfolio Capitalists in Central Asia

Anthony Jenkinson, author of the quotation that begins this chapter, was an agent of the Muscovy Company, an English joint-stock company chartered in 1555 to improve England's trade with Russia and, through Russia, with Asia. In the wake of Russia's annexation of the Khanates of Kazan in 1552 and Astrakhan in 1556 under Tsar Ivan IV ('the Terrible', r. 1547–84), Jenkinson left England for Moscow, and then travelled down the Volga River and across the Caspian Sea, reaching Bukhara in 1558. In addition to searching for an alternate route by which England could access the Indian Ocean trade, Jenkinson's account makes clear that he was acutely interested in the commercial climate of the states through which he passed. That said, Jenkinson was poorly informed of Central Asian customs and recent events in the region, and his mission was ultimately a failure. Additionally, he had the bad fortune to arrive at the end of a decades-long civil war that had weakened Bukharan political and economic structures. At the time, he had no way of knowing that his young Bukharan host, Abdullah Khan, would soon bring about an end to this civil war and advance a number of initiatives that would dramatically improve Bukhara's commercial infrastructure.

Jenkinson stayed in Bukhara for a little more than three months, during which time he tried to find traders interested in purchasing a portion of his stock of English kersey, a woolen cloth that, in the sixteenth century, was England's principal export commodity. Jenkinson's failure to find interested buyers was somewhat predictable, considering that he was trying to sell English wool in a region famous for its superior wool production. Jenkinson expressed a significant lack of enthusiasm for the Bukharan commercial climate at the time. Nevertheless, his account presents a number of interesting observations, including the fact that the merchants who arrived from India, Persia and elsewhere came there with 'great caravans' to attend the annual Bukharan trade fair, but that the Indians were so 'beggarly and poor' that they remained in Bukhara for two or even three years before returning home.

Revisiting Jenkinson's account in the context of the Multanis' commercial system, it seems that Jenkinson misunderstood the Indians' commercial activities in the Bukharan markets. Rather than languishing in Bukhara as they anxiously awaited merchants to come and buy their wares, Indian merchants had very good reasons to stay in the region for lengthy periods of time, frequently much longer than the 'two or three years' Jenkinson reported. Additionally, the Indians would have had very little motivation to purchase English wool, and even less to offer a reduced rate on the cotton cloth that they had transported to Bukhara by caravan. Rather than demonstrating the destitute nature of the Bukharan market at the time of his visit, Jenkinson's inability to purchase Indian cloth at a discounted price seems to suggest the saturation of the Bukharan market with Indian textiles and the efforts of the Multanis to keep the price of this commodity as high as possible.

In order to explain why this was so, we turn to the commercial system that the Indians used to develop their network in the region and maintain it for several centuries. At the heart of the Multani commercial presence in early modern Central Asia was the family firm, and at the heart of the Indian family firm was its reputation. For a firm to be successful, merchants from outside of the family needed to be able to trust that they could conduct business with the firm's agents in a predictable manner. Word spread quickly if a firm's reputation became tarnished. In such instances, affiliated agents would quickly find themselves unable to strike deals with other merchants, and they would lose access to sources of credit necessary to conduct their trade.

In their efforts to protect their reputations, firm directors needed to be able to monitor and even control the behaviour of their agents and their impulses to swindle, cheat, embezzle and even abscond with the firm's wealth. This would have been a serious challenge even for those agents working within the subcontinent, and the great distances, political boundaries and long periods of absence involved in the Indian merchants' trade in Central Asia would have made it seemingly impossible to manage. Nevertheless, the Multanis developed a system that enabled the firm directors to do just that.

Most importantly, a firm's senior agents were highly motivated to make certain that their junior colleagues operated in a way that reflected well on their firm. One finds evidence of only a few exceptional cases that involved agents converting to Islam, or Christianity (in Russia), or otherwise deliberately acting in a way that contravened the interests of the firm. One way that Indian firm directors were able to ensure that they could trust their agents was by recruiting them from within their caste when they were still young and putting them through long apprenticeships. Over many years, apprentices were trained in such critical areas as: accounting techniques; the distinctions among the many types of *hundi*s and their uses; methods to determine interest rates for a variety of types of loans and other moneylending procedures; legal issues that pertained to conducting business within their own legal traditions, and those of other communities; and secret numerical codes in use by the commercial communities. This training was critical to the merchants' success, and so was their affiliation to their firm as it provided access to the firm's capital, financial tools and resources. Without it, these exceptionally talented financial specialists would have been little more than small-time peddlers.

Upon completion of their training, firm directors loaned their agents a certain amount of capital, which they could use to begin building their portfolios. Two important features of these loans stand out. First, they were made at annual interest rates equal to approximately 10 per cent of the value of the capital. While such a rate may seem high, we will see that it was quite reasonable when one considers the returns that the agents were able to realize on the initial investment. A second important feature of these loans is that, rather than cash, they were generally made in kind, and most commonly in cotton textiles. This is corroborated by the large number of observers who identify Multani merchants in Central Asia, Iran and elsewhere as traders in cotton textiles.

Such an arrangement was both shrewd and logical, when one considers what we know of the Multanis' commercial networks within India, discussed above. Recall that Multani networks in India were deeply involved in financing the agricultural production of cotton and its transportation to regional markets. Leveraging their commercial relationships with the weaving communities to whom they provided raw materials, the Multani firms enjoyed access to abundant supplies of cotton textiles at below-wholesale prices. At the same time, our sources indicate that there was a considerable and sustained demand for these same textiles in Central Asian markets. In Central Asia, Indian cloth was as good as silver.

In order to arrange the movement of these materials to their destinations in Central Asia, groups of Multani agents contracted with Afghan nomads, Lohanis and others. For several months the Multani agents travelled with Powinda caravans as they lumbered across treacherous and inhospitable territories, loading the camels every morning and unloading them every evening. While the journey was an arduous one, travel with Powindas would have been considerably safer than trying to navigate the journey without them. Not only did the Afghans know the best routes to travel, but they were a formidable force unto themselves, able to provide excellent security.

Interior of an Indian Caravanserai in Bukhara (1890s)

Upon arriving in Central Asia, the Multanis would take up residence in one of several locations. In general, Muslim Multanis lived in caravanserais or other residences alongside other non-Indian Muslims. Hindus, however, lived in their own dedicated caravanserais, which were commonly owned by other Indians.

Within the walls of their caravanserais, the Hindus were exempt from many of the legal restrictions that applied to local peoples. Visitors to these caravanserais reported, for example, that within their richly decorated walls Indians were permitted to smoke and consume alcohol, activities that were prohibited for the local Central Asian Muslim population. They were also permitted to celebrate religious festivals, such as Diwali and Holi. These celebrations reportedly included the use of alcohol and narcotics, and it is perhaps not surprising that they occasionally became rambunctious, causing some friction with the local population and requiring the interference of the authorities. In other instances, however, local Central Asians joined in the Hindus' celebrations, bringing cows to the caravanserais on Diwali, for example, so the merchants could feed them cottonseed and sprinkle dye on them while they prayed.

Indians in a Smoking Room in Bukhara (1880s)

Hindu Indians could also freely engage in their religious practices within the confines of their caravanserais. Family-firm directors facilitated this by enlisting Brahmins to travel even to the most distant locations, so that they could administer religious rites and ceremonies for their agents. Like the merchants themselves, Brahmins circulated throughout the diaspora, generally serving for several years before being relieved by a replacement.

In a small number of locations in Afghanistan and Iran, the Brahmins were stationed at free-standing temples. One such location was a reportedly ancient

Indians in Bukhara (1880s)

Jawalamukhi temple to the goddess Durga, located near Baku, Azerbaijan, and built on top of naphtha deposits that belched flame from the earth. But the existence of actual temples outside of India was exceptional. Most often Brahmins in Central Asia resided in the Indian caravanserais, where they supervised religious ceremonies in dedicated temple rooms.

Outside of the caravanserais, Hindus (as was the case for Jews, Christians and other minority groups) were required to submit to a number of restrictions. They were forbidden from riding horses within the city walls, for example, and they were required to dress in a distinctive manner so the Muslim populace could readily recognize them. Alexander Burnes summarizes:

> They are not permitted to build temples, nor set up idols, nor walk in procession: they do not ride within the walls of the city, and must wear a peculiar dress. They pay the 'jizyu,' or poll-tax, which varies from four to eight rupees a year; but this they only render in common with others, not Mahommedans. They must never abuse or ill-use a Mahommedan. When the king passes their quarter of the city, they must draw up, and wish him health and prosperity; when on horseback outside the city, they must dismount if they meet his majesty or the Cazee. They are not permitted to purchase female slaves, as an infidel would defile a believer; nor do any of them bring their families beyond the Oxus. For these sacrifices the Hindoos in Bokhara live unmolested, and, in all trials and suits, have equal justice with the Mahommedans. I could hear of no forcible instance of conversion to Islam, though three or four individuals had changed their creed in as many years. The deportment of these people is most sober and orderly;—one would imagine that the tribe had renounced laughter, if he judged by the gravity of their countenances.

They themselves, however, speak highly of their privileges, and are satisfied at the celerity with which they can realise money, though it be at the sacrifice of their prejudices.[5]

One recurrent cause of friction was the cremation ceremony that the Hindus held when a member of their community died. While this ceremony was standard within India, local populations elsewhere found it abhorrent, and they expressed great discomfort at the notion of human ashes making their way into the air and water. But the Indians were adamant that they must be permitted to cremate their dead, and with only a few temporary exceptions their hosts granted them permission. Bukharan Amirs were even known to have provided a military escort to ensure that disgruntled locals would not disrupt the ceremony. After the ceremony the ashes of the deceased were gathered so they could be returned to India.

Once established within their caravanserais, the Indians would store their merchandise and begin to sell, piece by piece, the bolts of cloth that their firm directors had credited to them. If the market demand were exceptional, one could imagine the Multanis quickly selling their merchandise. But when one considers that each caravan that made its way from India to Central

Indian Cremation Ceremony in Bukhara (1880s)

Asia included hundreds, or even thousands, of camel-loads of cloth, this seems unlikely. To do so would have flooded the market, causing a dramatic drop in the value of their capital, and the capital of all of the other Indians in the region. Rather, it was in the Indians' best interest to sell their merchandise gradually in order to keep the price as high as possible. This required Multani merchants to spend several years in Central Asia—seven or eight years seems to have been the average—during which time they engaged in a variety of commercial activities, only one facet of which was selling Indian textiles.

The more senior agents, many of whom spent decades away from India, were charged with supervising all the agents' commercial activities and ensuring that new arrivals conducted their trade in a way that benefited the entire community. As new agents arrived with caravans and others departed for home at the end of a long tenure away, packets full of *hundi*s and letters full of secretive information also moved between the distant communities and the principal investors in India. At its core, the Indian network was maintained through the circulation of men, merchandise, wealth and information between Multan and many dozens of distant satellites.

It was, of course, necessary for new arrivals to sell some of their cloth in order to begin engaging in other commercial activities, the most important of which was advancing loans for interest. Here, we again emphasize that the Multanis' trade had little in common with the standard peddler model of buying cheap, transporting far and selling dear, and doing the same on the return journey. Rather, these were highly trained financial specialists who sought every opportunity to keep their capital profitably invested the full time they were abroad. As soon as they retrieved capital from a sale, the Multanis were busy at work reinvesting it in other ventures. It was not uncommon for a Multani who had sold his initial capital investment to choose to completely leave behind the buying and selling of merchandise in favour of the highly profitable moneylending trade.

The loans that the Indians advanced generally fell into one of two categories: cash loans made against collateral, and agricultural loans made against a future harvest. Cash loans were made according to one of a number of repayment schedules, which varied depending upon the nature of the loan, the risk involved and the maximum rate permitted by local law. The general model is one in which the Multani would deliver a certain amount of money to a debtor to be repaid on a weekly basis for a period of time that would earn the lender a profit. For example, a typical contract might stipulate that a loan of ten tanga be repaid at the rate of two tanga per week for six weeks, earning the lender a profit of two tanga. While that represents a small sum, engaging one's capital in such a venture extended over a year amounted to more than 160 per cent annual interest. Another example required a debtor who had taken a loan of twenty tanga to repay the lender thirty tanga within a two-month term, amounting to an annual interest rate of 300 per cent. As will be discussed in chapter seven, in later years the Russian colonial administration enforced severe restrictions on the Indians' moneylending business. So when the American diplomat Eugene Schuyler visited the Indian community in Tashkent in the 1870s, he found that 'the Hindoos usually lend sums for twenty-four weeks, to be paid in weekly installments of one *tenga* to every *tilla*, that is one nineteenth, making a gain as interest in the course of the transaction of five *tengas*, or about twenty-six percent., which would be fully fifty-six per cent. per annum'.[6]

Because many Central Asian farmers required some form of rural credit to plant their crops, agricultural loans were essential for the farmers and a lucrative venture for Indian merchants in Central Asia. These loans generally followed the same pattern in Central Asia that they did in India: the Indian moneylender advanced farmers a loan prior to the planting season and collected the proceeds at harvest time. The moneylenders commonly took their payment as a percentage of the harvest, and, as in India, they are also known to have purchased the remainder of the crop for cash. Again, this was an especially valuable service for local governments as it served to monetize local economies, which facilitated the collection of taxes in cash.

This helps explain why Central Asian rulers would go to such great lengths to welcome Hindus in their realms, offer them protection, and ensure that they could safely conduct their trade in a predictable environment. Nevertheless, the local population frequently found the Indians' business tactics to be very shrewd and they resented the fact that the Indians enjoyed governmental support. The Bukharan administration's policy of protecting the Indians' commercial interest, despite a popular tradition portraying them as exploitative usurers, is clearly expressed in the early eighteenth-century invective launched by Mir Muhammad Amin Bukhari, the author of the 'Ubaydullahnama:

Indian people were masters above Muslims. In trade relations they, stain upon stain, lawlessly put Muslims through one unpleasantry after another. If, for example, a Muslim man in this [moneylending] trade showed some slowness, so the Hindu would send his 'horse of pride' to the Muslim and nobody could find out how and why. If a Muslim appealed with a claim to a Hindu, or a Hindu to a Muslim, so a protector would defend the Hindu and decide the affair not according to the law, but simply according to the order of the baltu-i serai, and the property of the Muslim would be taken by force. If such an offense was proven, and people told the Khan about this, then his servants would show facts to be contrary. In these cases Muslims began to appeal for fairness to the true ruler, demanding strong retribution to the Kafir-Indians from Allah.[7]

A century and a half later, the Hungarian scholar and traveller Arminius Vámbéry visited Bukhara and found the situation little changed. In Vámbéry's words: 'as the pious Kadi for the most part carries on business in common with the worshipper of Vishnoo, it is rarely that the victim (debtor) escapes'.[8]

Moneylending was arguably the most important part of the Indian merchants' commercial portfolios, but it was not the only part. During their long years away from home, many Indians combined their moneylending ventures with a variety of other investments. The list would have been a long one, but chief among them were limited commercial partnerships with other Indians or local merchants, and lending money or materials to handicraft producers in the area in exchange for a part of the finished product. Such ventures could be exceptionally profitable in their own right.

As a rule, Indian merchants in Central Asia would have kept their capital invested at all times, right up to the moment of departure. Doing so ensured that they would maximize the profits from their years abroad, and keeping money invested was also much safer than gathering proceeds in cash. At the last moment, one could always find a colleague willing to purchase active loan contracts for cash or credit. The agent could then convert his wealth into a *hundi*, which would be safer than travelling with a large amount of cash and which he could convert back into cash in Multan. Merchants might also use their wealth, or some part of it, to purchase horses or other merchandise abundant in Central Asia and in demand in India. But while an outside observer might mistakenly characterize the Multanis as peddlers, moving textiles to Central Asia and horses to India, for example, this trade was only a small part of their financial portfolio.

On returning home, the agents presented themselves to their investors, the firm directors, who put them through a grand financial reckoning. The agents were required to produce their *bahis*, the account books that detailed every transaction that they made and every expense that they had incurred during their time away. Entries in these books would include such line items as the nature of the initial loan the director had provided to the agent and the terms of that loan; proceeds from selling the merchandise that constituted that loan; any payments that had been made against that loan; all of the loans that the agent had issued, and the proceeds from those loans; any existing accounts left with colleagues in the region; income or financial transfers made by *hundi*; living expenses that had been incurred abroad; expenses incurred in arranging for transport; and any advances that the firm directors would have provided to an individual agent's wife and children to help sustain them during the agent's long absence.

In settling their accounts, the agents repaid their creditor for all expenses and the appropriate interest. After having been away from home for several years and working tirelessly the whole time to keep the firm's capital invested in an array of profitable ventures, the agents would have had to turn over a substantial part of the profits to the firm. Recall that the firm directors had, after all, trained the agent, provided the initial investment, used their influence to arrange for safe travel and transportation to Central Asia by Powinda caravan, and assumed considerable financial risk.

Still, there was plenty of profit to go around. Even agents who started off with little or no capital investment of their own stood to make an extraordinarily large amount of money in this trade. While many stayed in Central Asia for a few years before returning home, some made return trips, and others are known to have stayed in particularly desirable locations for decades. The most successful used their wealth, knowledge and position to begin their own firms, with their own apprentices.

On to Shikarpur

The image of the Indian commercial system presented above emphasizes its stability. To a great extent this is warranted, as evidenced by the Indians' sustained operation in Central Asian urban centres and the agrarian countryside over several centuries. But there were, of course, changes over time. The Multani commercial system exhibited considerable flexibility, with agents venturing into new regions in pursuit of emerging opportunities, and abandoning long-established communities when opportunities there evaporated. Unpredictable circumstances also occasionally led to dramatic and abrupt changes in the commercial network as a whole. We will discuss several of these in the next chapter. One, however, directly relates to the continuity and composition of the Indian communities in early modern Central Asia, and so we will address it directly.

During the latter half of the eighteenth century, the identity of the majority of the Indian merchants in Central Asia changed from the age-old Multani to a new designation, Shikarpuri. This reflected a shift in the commercial centre of gravity in north-west India away from Multan in favour of Shikarpur, a small town in northern Sind that had been established in the sixteenth century as a hunting retreat. To some extent, this might be considered a change in name alone, insofar as many of the very Multani families who had dispatched agents to Central Asia throughout the seventeenth century remained engaged in the same trade, only from a new location and now identified as Shikarpuris. Recounting his experiences in the region during the 1820s and '30s, Charles Masson was a proponent of this view:

> As the city [Shikarpur] is not understood to be one of great antiquity, it is possible that the influx of Hindús to it is not of very distant date, and that it was occasioned by the fluctuations of political power. As the existence of some great centre of monetary transactions, in this part of the world, was always indispensable for the facilities of the commerce carried on in it, it is not unlikely, looking at the facts within our knowledge connected with the condition of the adjacent country during the last two centuries, that Múltân preceded Shikárpúr as the great money mart, and that from it the Hindús removed, converting the insignificant village of the chace [hinterland] into a city of the first rate and consequence.[9]

According to Masson, at that time, Shikarpur had emerged as 'the great money-mart of Central Asia', taking for itself the role that Multan had served in the past. At about the same time, in 1831, Alexander Burnes

similarly found that Shikarpuris had risen to dominate
the financial industry in the region to such an extent
that they even had agents stationed in Multan, where
he reportedly came across 'forty Shroffs, chiefly natives
of Shikarpoor'.[10]

There is some truth to the notion that the
Shikarpuris who became so ubiquitous in Central Asia
and Afghanistan in the late eighteenth and nineteenth
centuries were in actuality simply Multanis operating
under a different name. But this is only part of the
story. At the same time as large numbers of Multanis
migrated to Shikarpur, the new opportunities that
Shikarpur presented attracted other commercial
families from throughout the region, especially from
Sind. These were families that previously had not
engaged in trans-regional commerce, but now began
to do so. What genuinely remained the same is that, as
had been the case in Multan, during the late eighteenth
and nineteenth centuries, Shikarpur developed into
what Claude Markovits aptly described as a sort of
Bania 'melting pot'.[11] Khatri families who had formerly
been known as Multanis now became Shikarpuris, as
did many others with multiple caste affiliations. One
finds an additional layer of complexity in that not all
of the Multani firms abandoned their ancestral home.
Some remained in Multan and continued to dispatch

agents to Central Asia, where they were still identified as Multanis.

The degree to which the Shikarpuri and Multani family firms were of the same ancestry remains debatable. But the dominant role that Shikarpuris came to play in mediating India's commercial relationship with Central Asia from the late eighteenth century onwards is quite clear. When he visited Shikarpur in the 1830s, Mohan Lal, the astute and well-travelled Kashmiri companion to Alexander Burnes, expressed genuine astonishment:

> I feasted my eyes with the beauty of the bazar at Shikarpur. After passing through lanes closely peopled, I stepped into the large bazar, and found it full. There was no shop in which I did not observe half a dozen Khatri merchants, who appeared to me to have no time to speak to the purchasers. Such was the briskness of trade going on in the bazar . . . It occurred to me that the reason why Shikarpur surpasses Amritsar in wealth is, that its inhabitants, who are for the most part Khatris, have spread themselves in almost all the regions of Central Asia, whence they return loaded with gains to their families at Shikarpur. There is not so much commerce carried on at Shikarpur, I believe,

as in Multan and Amritsar, but you will see all the shopkeepers writing Hoondees, or bills of exchange, which you can take in the name of their agents at Bombay, Sindh, the Panjab, Khorasan, Afghanistan, part of Persia, and Russia.[12]

Several factors led to a deterioration of the commercial climate in Multan in the eighteenth century, and the corresponding rise of Shikarpur. The most important of these was a loss of confidence in Multan's stability as a financial centre. Throughout the Delhi Sultanate and Mughal eras, and even into the early decades of the eighteenth century, Multan had prospered as a valued and well-defended commercial asset. As the Mughal hold over the city weakened, especially following Nadir Shah's infamous 1739 invasion of India and sack of Delhi, Multan fell prey to a number of vying interests. Over the course of the period between 1749 and 1849, Multan was invaded by Afghan, Maratha, Sikh and then finally British armies. By the beginning of the nineteenth century, the city had lost its status as one of the great financial markets of the early modern world.

At the same time, Shikarpur rose to greatness. This appears to have been partly a result of the single-most traumatic event in Multanis' long history in

early modern Iran. As Safavid power waned, a Ghilzai
Afghan tribal confederation invaded Iran in 1722 and
occupied Isfahan, capital of the empire and home to
the largest population of Multanis outside of India. An
Armenian observer of the Ghilzai invasion, Petros di
Sarkis Gilanentz, reported that the Afghans demanded
that the Multanis produce 25,000 tomans to secure
their safety. Because their capital was invested and not
readily available in cash, the Indians were only able
to produce 20,000 tomans. According to Gilanentz's
account the Afghans responded violently, decimating
the Indian communities. After it was all done:

> Only a few Indians were left in the town; these
> people had advanced money to the Muhammadans
> against promissory notes (*sanad*) and jewels, gold,
> silver and house ornaments (*zinat*). Mahmud took
> all these valuables from them without payment,
> not even regarding them as forming part of their
> indemnity. The shops of those Multanis who had
> died or had fled were consequently closed, but
> Mahmud had them opened and seized all their
> contents.[13]

Even after Nadir Shah (r. 1736–47) removed the
Ghilzai threat and usurped the throne from his Safavid

patrons, he retained policies hostile to Indians in his territory. Nadir Shah declared the Indians' status to be unprotected, and he used that decision as an excuse to confiscate their wealth and property. By the time Nadir Shah was assassinated in 1747, the once-great Multani communities of Iran were gone.

In the wake of such devastation, the Multani firms found great solace in the rise to power of Ahmad Khan of the Abdali tribe (r. 1747–72), Nadir Shah's successor in Afghanistan. Upon his ascension to a regal position at the age of twenty-five, Ahmad was restyled Ahmad Shah Durrani, a shortened form of *Durr-i Durran*, or 'Pearl of Pearls': possibly a reference to his tendency to wear a pearl earring. Ahmad Shah declared the sovereign independence of his territory, Afghanistan, and he established a new Durrani capital in the city of Qandahar. Focusing his attention eastwards, towards the realm that he saw to be his inherited right from Nadir Shah, Ahmad Shah and his tribal coalition clashed with the armies of the Mughals, Marathas and Sikhs. He extended his territory deep into Baluchistan and Sind, conquered much of the Punjab and Kashmir, and annexed northern Afghanistan up to the Amu Darya River.

Ahmad Shah Durrani reversed Nadir Shah's shortsighted and predatory policies towards Indian merchants. Instead of persecution, Ahmad Shah encouraged Indians to settle in Afghanistan and he used their trans-regional trade connections for the benefit of his young state. From Ahmad Shah's reign, Hindu merchants became closely intertwined with the Durrani government. They are known to have purchased the rights to collect transit taxes on behalf of the Durranis, they extended loans to government officials, and they were even appointed to high positions in the state's financial administration.

The close relationship that the Indian firms shared with the Durrani administration, as well as their need to maintain a close working relationship with the Powinda nomads, helps explain why the Multanis, and others, chose to make the move from Multan to Shikarpur, a Durrani possession. Merchants found the city's location agreeable, as it was situated in Sind near the Indus River and along trade routes leading through the Bolan Pass and on to Qandahar, the first Durrani capital. But above all, the Shikarpuri firms found themselves well protected, and able to pursue commercial ventures in Afghanistan and Central Asia under the auspices of the Durrani state. In the wake of the complete dislocation of the Multani network in Safavid territories, Ahmad Shah's encouragement represented a tangible motivation for the Multanis to relocate to the safety and security of Shikarpur, and they did so in large numbers.

5. INDIAN TEXTILES

It ought to be remembered that the whole of the merchandise which is exported from the Mogul kingdom comes from four kinds of plants—that is to say, the shrub that produces the cotton from which a large quantity of cloth, coarse and fine, is made. These cotton goods are exported to Europe, Persia, Arabia, and other quarters of the world. The second is the plant which produces indigo. The third is the one from which comes opium, of which a large amount is used on the Java coast. The fourth is the mulberry-tree, on which their silk-worms are fed, and, as it may be said, that commodity (silk) is grown on those trees. For the export of all this merchandise, European and other traders bring much silver to India.[1]

—Niccolao Manucci, c.1707

We have seen above that early modern Indian and Central Asian rulers maintained a keen appreciation for the roles that trans-regional trade played in their economies. Thus, even during periods of political tension, rulers on both side worked to ensure that the trade routes between them remained open and safe for passage, and that the caravan traders who travelled these routes could conduct their trade in a predictable environment. Rulers had good reason to support these traders. In addition to offering valuable financial services in both urban and rural markets, traders strengthened the state's economy by exchanging surplus merchandise for commodities that were in demand at home and available in abundance elsewhere.

The focus of the next three chapters will shift to several of the most important commodities dealt with by the Multanis, Powindas and other caravan traders involved in India's trade with Central Asia. Our sources make repeated references to fine silks, furs and other luxury goods, which are comparatively easier to locate in the historical record as they were destined for consumption by the wealthy elite—those most likely to appear in the published chronicles and other historical sources. But in both quantity and value the overwhelming majority of the merchandise that moved along the caravan routes were bulk goods, loaded onto carts or strapped to the backs of camels, horses, donkeys and bullocks. Both India and Central Asia excelled at producing certain types of commodities that enjoyed sustained demand far beyond their borders, and the reasons for this had much to do with geography, climate and other environmental factors.

In India, cotton textiles were far and away the most important export during the early modern era. Niccolao Manucci (1639–1717), an Italian traveller and physician who spent the majority of his life in Mughal India, observes as much in the quotation that begins this chapter. Textiles are followed by indigo and other dyes; sugar, both raw and refined from sugar cane; bulk quantities of Indian rice, which was considered superior to Central Asian varieties; precious stones and jewellery; weapons; and, of course, spices, including pepper, cinnamon, nutmeg, mace, cloves and ginger. To this one can add bulk shipments of tea, beginning in the early nineteenth century. Other sources illustrate the importance of the slave trade throughout the medieval and early modern eras, as large numbers of Indians were captured, enslaved and then transported by caravan to markets beyond the boundaries of the subcontinent. Many of these individuals were ultimately sold in the Central Asian slave markets.

On the Central Asian side, textile imports were largely offset by the annual exportation of tens of thousands of horses, bred by pastoral nomadic peoples inhabiting the open grasslands of the Inner Asian steppe of modern Kazakhstan and Siberia. The horse trade was by far the most important component of the Central Asian commercial economy, followed by the trade in Central Asian fruits, both fresh and dried, and a number of other, less important commodities such as silk and paper. Manucci and other observers suggest that, on the whole, Indian merchants generally enjoyed a favourable balance of trade with foreign merchants, and it was common to settle their accounts with gold or silver, commodities that were in high demand in the subcontinent. For their part, foreign merchants were quite content to trade precious metals for merchandise in India, as it equipped them with greater purchasing power than they would have in other markets that boasted richer natural precious metal reserves.

Indian Cottons

Indians have been cultivating cotton, spinning it into yarn and weaving it into fabric for clothing since the Bronze Age. Textile fragments excavated at Mohenjo Daro indicate that, four thousand years ago, local producers were already processing dyes to decorate their clothing. Early Greek written sources, including

Herodotus, provide multiple references to Indian cottons, identifying them among the most popular import commodities in Greek markets. Demand both within India and foreign markets spurred production, and well before the beginning of the Common Era Indians in several regions of the subcontinent had developed extensive cotton cultivation and textile production industries.

In the years around the beginning of the Common Era, the Romans appear to have been somewhat preoccupied with Indian textiles, which they favoured for their flowing white togas and other fine clothes. Indian cottons were cooler to wear in the Mediterranean summer than wool or linen, and as an exotic import they were considered a mark of distinction, indicating the high social status of the wearer. Referencing Rome's severe trade deficit vis-à-vis India, the Roman historian, Pliny the Elder (23–79 CE), sniped, 'In no year does India drain our empire of less than five hundred and fifty millions of sesterces [coins], giving back her own wares in exchange, which are sold among us at fully one hundred times their prime cost'.[2] Writing at nearly the same time, the anonymous author of the *Periplus Maris Erithraei*, a guidebook for Roman mariners in the Indian Ocean, identifies the ancient port of Barygaza, located near modern Mumbai, as the optimal location to purchase these coveted Indian textiles. The *Periplus* similarly emphasizes the magnitude of Rome's trade deficit with India, and the paramount importance of Indian cottons in that trade.[3]

Several factors contributed to the gradual development of India's cotton textile industry. The most significant among these was the Indian climate, with long summers of abundant sunshine coupled with abundant water supplies to irrigate the rich soils. Indian crops received water from several sources. In addition to the monsoons, which provided weeks of heavy rains, Indian farmers took advantage of multiple expansive river networks fed throughout long, hot summers by snowmelt, especially from the Himalayas but also from other mountain ranges. From antiquity, this enabled Indian farmers to produce ample food supplies, which supported the development of a large agrarian population able to direct substantial effort to cotton production both for domestic consumption and for export.

In the early modern era, the population of India was second only to that of China. Estimates vary, but it seems reasonable to accept that the total population of the Indian subcontinent in 1600 was close to 150 million. As was the case in nearly the entire pre-industrial world, some 80 to 90 per cent of the population lived in villages and made a living by growing crops and raising livestock. Much of their effort focused on growing grains and other foodstuffs, but cotton production grew apace. During the Mughal era, this expansion was further supported by state policies that rewarded farmers for growing a variety of cash crops for export to foreign markets. These included indigo, sugar, opium and especially cotton, which was grown in abundance across the subcontinent and woven into hundreds of millions of yards of cloth. Today, there is every reason to accept the economic historian K. N. Chaudhuri's assertion, made some four decades ago, that, prior to the Industrial Revolution, 'the Indian subcontinent was probably the world's greatest producer of cotton textiles'.[4]

Of course, textile production in India required much more than just growing cotton. The transformation of that cotton into an extraordinary array of finished textiles also involved farmers who grew dyes, spinners who turned the raw cotton into yarn of various qualities, weavers who turned the yarn into bolts of cloth, and printers who decorated the cloth and prepared it for sale. While the rich resources and dense populations of the north Indian Punjab and Doab regions may have enjoyed some advantage in developing an integrated system of cotton textile production, south Indian producers did not lag behind.

Across the subcontinent, Indian farmers, weavers
and merchants collaborated to produce hundreds
of types of cotton textiles. These varieties can be
differentiated based on such factors as the location of
production; the type of weave; the thickness of the
cotton; and whether spinners had blended it with linen,
silk or other fibres. Indians produced simple calicos,
printed chintzes in most every imaginable design,
elegant gauze-like muslins, and more.

The Indian textile producers' neighbours in Iran
and Central Asia developed their own textile industries,
but these were negligible compared to the Indian
industry. To be sure, Iranian and Central Asian weavers
did produce certain special varieties that enjoyed
considerable international demand. The Central Asian
textile known as *zandanichi*—a finely woven blend of
cotton and silk—is known to have been exported even
to India, for example. But apart from special varieties,
Indian production was far greater than anything that
the smaller populations in Iran or Central Asia were
capable of, and Indians were able to exploit their
significantly greater resources and more suitable
environment to bring their textiles to market at more
competitive prices. Thus, in the seventeenth century,
the French traveller Jean Chardin visited both Persia
and India and concluded that, while the Persians were

able to produce some textiles, they had no motivation to expand production as they were able to get more and better varieties from India at cheaper prices.[5]

Working through the early modern historical sources, one finds that many European merchants took an interest in the Indian cotton textile export trade. While the figures pertaining to this trade that the European observers advance appear to be impressively precise, one must keep in mind that they are essentially rough estimates. They very likely fail to take into account significant portions of Indian production, unaccounted-for smuggling, and even false data filed by lazy East India Company employees. We therefore cannot claim that the available figures are in any way precise. But they are useful to us insofar as they provide an impressionistic sense of the general magnitude of the caravan trade in Indian textiles.

Throughout the course of the seventeenth century, European records refer to Indian cotton farmers, weavers, dyers and merchants across the subcontinent. The textiles that were produced for export markets, however, were generally produced in one of four key regions: Bengal, the Coromandel Coast, Gujarat, and the north-west (the Punjab, Multan and Sind). Figures for the early decades of the seventeenth century are significantly more modest than those towards the end

of the century. Thus, English reports from the 1620s
suggest that the Company was selling roughly 250,000
pieces of Indian cloth in London each year. As each
piece of cloth was approximately ten yards in length,
that translates to 2.5 million yards of cloth. By the 1680s,
the figures appear to have increased substantially, with
English exports of Indian cloth reaching an estimated
18 million yards. While these estimates are admittedly
unreliable, they do indicate that European textile
exports from India were substantial and on a generally
upward trend throughout the seventeenth century.
Still, European consumption represented only some
10 per cent of India's total production, the vast majority
of which went to India's own consumers and other
non-European markets.

In terms of the caravan trade with Central Asia and
Persia, the majority of the textiles to have been loaded
into bullock carts or strapped to the backs of camels,
donkeys or other pack animals were produced in the
Punjab and Sind. Muzaffar Alam has noted that this
trade was robust during the Mughal era, and that it
contributed to a significant increase in urbanization
in north-western India, the rise of a highly effective
portfolio capitalist commercial culture, and the
development of considerable new textile production
centres in towns such as Lahore, Bajwara, Batal,

Machhiwara, Samana and Sialkot.[6] It is reasonable to assume that the majority of the textiles exported to Central Asian markets, and onwards from there, originated in the Punjab and Sind. But Central Asian sources occasionally refer to other textile varieties by name, such as '*chit-i porband*', which is probably a reference to cloth made in the vicinity of Porbandar, in Gujarat. In another Central Asian source, the *Dastur al-Muluk*, the author Samander Termizi describes an instance in which a bolt of Gujarati cloth was spread beneath the feet of the Bukharan ruler Subhan Quli Khan (r. 1681–1702), honouring him on his arrival to the city of Qarshi.

This is instructive, but it says little about the quantity of textiles annually transported to the region and sold in Central Asian markets. Before examining the evidence, it is worthwhile first to direct our attention to a few of the logistical details associated with the caravan trade. Early modern sources refer to caravans in a wide variety of contexts. In the excerpt at the beginning of the first chapter, for example, Babur refers to an annual movement of between ten and twenty thousand pack animals making their way from India to Kabul, loaded with textiles and a variety of other merchandise. In his account, Babur is careful to differentiate caravan traffic bound for Central Asia from the traffic that passed through Qandahar en route to markets in Persia and further to the west.

European accounts of the seventeenth century suggest that, even during the period of European ascendancy in the Indian Ocean, between 25,000 and 30,000 camels annually transported Indian merchandise—principally cotton textiles—along the overland trade routes from Qandahar to Isfahan. Considering that the standard camels used in India carried loads that weighed in excess of 400 pounds, these figures suggest that Indian traders supplied Iranian markets with more than 5000 tons of merchandise each year. Converting pounds of cloth to yards, we find that this amounts to some 72 million yards of cloth, an amount sufficient to clothe the entire population of the Safavid Empire. Thus, in 1618, one English traveller to Iran asserted that Indians were 'the chief merchants who vend linen of India of all sorts and prices which this country cannot be without, except the people should go naked'. Despite a temporary disruption during the tumultuous second quarter of the eighteenth century, this trade continued well into the nineteenth century. Much the same can be said for Central Asia.

In the wake of Babur's establishment of the Mughal Empire, multiple sources refer to the large-scale movement of Indian cottons through Kabul to Central

Asia. We find references to many different types of Indian textiles in Central Asian markets. These include: Kashmiri shawls; small handkerchiefs; larger pieces of cloth for turbans, towels and robes; Banarasi wraps; silk brocade; linens; as well as muslin, calico and chintz produced in a wide variety of qualities and patterns in the north-west and exported in bulk quantities. For example, the will of Tangri Berdi, a wealthy Central Asian merchant who died in the year 1589 in Samarqand, lists among the property in his estate 429 pieces of Indian cloth.[7] Four decades later, in 1639, the English explorer Henry Bornford undertook a journey from Agra to the port of Tatta in Sind. He identified Lahore as the recipient of nearly all of the cotton production in the region and the prime commercial centre in the Punjab, especially as it related to the trade with Uzbek Central Asia. He summarizes that, in Lahore, these goods 'are bought by the Wousbecks [Uzbeks] or Tartarrs and soe transported by Cabull into those parts'.[8] Only the chintz produced farther to the south in Samana was not part of this trade, as it was transported to Persian markets by the overland route through Qandahar.

Recalling the earlier discussion of the state's interest in supporting trans-regional trade, we find that the Bukharan nobility worked to promote the textile trade by writing letters on behalf of trans-regional traders, albeit indirectly, and they even participated in the trade themselves through gift exchanges. In 1620–21, the Mughal Emperor Jahangir sent a letter to Sheikh Taj al-Din Hassan, the leader of the highly influential Juybari Sufi order in Bukhara, in which he writes that he had entrusted his ambassador with a gift of cotton cloth and other merchandise for the Sheikh, which was valued at 50,000 khanis. In another letter, we find that Shah Jahan, Jahangir's son and successor, had his ambassador to Balkh deliver some 600 pieces of red calico as a gift for Nadir Muhammad, the Astrakhanid ruler of that city. That same year, Nadir Muhammad reportedly held a banquet to honour his brother, Imam Quli Khan, ruler of Bukhara, and distributed gifts to his guests that included hundreds of Indian turbans and other pieces of Indian cloth. Also during Shah Jahan's reign, a diplomatic letter from Bukhara requests that a Bukharan merchant, Khwaja Awaz, be permitted to send his subordinate agents to Kabul in order to purchase Indian cloth.[9] Another diplomatic letter sent from Bukhara to a Mughal emperor, probably Aurangzeb, appeals that the rulers protect traders moving between their regions and requests that the Mughals assist the Bukharan merchant entrusted with delivering the letter so that he might acquire Indian textiles, explaining, 'at this time textiles are difficult to find in the boundaries of Bukhara'.[10]

Before moving on to other commodities, it is important to emphasize that India's trade with Central Asia was by no means a 'terminal' trade. That is to say, while many of the items transported to Central Asian markets were for local consumption in the region, others were part of a vast transit trade that moved Indian products onwards to markets in Siberia, China, Muscovy and beyond. Just as one finds Indian cloth moving through Iran to northern markets, one finds many sources that refer to Bukharan traders transporting large quantities of textiles to trade partners beyond their borders. Although the sources are generally silent about the origins of these textiles, considering the evidence it seems likely that many, if not most, of these textiles originated in India.

6.   THE SLAVE TRADE

> *The booty amounted in gold and silver, rubies and pearls, nearly to three thousand thousand (three million) dirhams, and the number of prisoners may be conceived from the fact that each was sold for from two to ten dirhams. These were afterwards taken to Ghazna, and merchants came from distant cities to purchase them, so that the countries of Mawarannahr (Central Asia), Iraq and Khurasan were filled with them, and the fair and the dark, the rich and the poor, mingled in one common slavery.*[1]

—al-Utbi, c.1020

Alongside textiles, Indian slaves were another commodity that was already in high demand in Central Asian markets during the medieval era. The historian

Abu Nasr Muhammad al-Utbi wrote his *Tarikh al-Yamini* as a history of the early Ghaznavid rulers, focusing especially on Mahmud (r. 998–1030), the Turkic ruler of Ghazna whose predecessors had served as elite military slaves and commanders to the Samanid Amirs in Bukhara (819–1005). Turkic troops stationed on the Samanids' eastern frontier raided Indian settlements and temples prior to Mahmud's reign, but as the Samanid regime weakened and toppled, Mahmud institutionalized these raids. Mahmud led a total of seventeen campaigns into India, returning to his capital of Ghazna with immense wealth and untold numbers of people taken into slavery, earning the title, 'Hammer of the Infidels'.

Our present interest is focused on the enslavement of Indians (non-Muslims or, less commonly, Muslims who were adherents to sects that their political opponents deemed to be heretical) during the early modern era and their exportation to foreign markets. But several features of this trade should be emphasized. First, the institution of slavery long predated the earliest Islamic rule in India, it continued even into the British colonial era, and despite it being illegal, in certain forms it continues even today. Indigenous Indian sources such as the Arthashastra, the Manu-smriti, the Mahabharata all refer to institutionalized slavery in India. Other sources suggest that it existed as a legally regulated institution as early as the Vedic period. Considering India in the context of the premodern world, the fact that slavery was legally sanctioned should come as no surprise. One can identify variations in legal definitions and rights, but the institution of slavery was present in virtually every ancient civilization. In this regard, India simply was not an exception.

Enslavement

The excerpt that opens this chapter describes events in 1018–19, following Mahmud's victory over Mathura during his twelfth campaign into India. While al-Utbi's account deserves some credence due to his position as secretary to Mahmud, we must also recognize that it very likely suffers from exaggeration. Scholars who have compared al-Utbi's chronicle with other contemporary sources have found that he included many errors in fact and he seems to have a penchant for exaggeration, especially when he thought it might serve to enhance his patron's image as a powerful Muslim commander relentlessly bent on expanding the boundaries of the Dar al-Islam. We know that al-Utbi did not accompany Mahmud on this campaign, and, taking the context of authorship into consideration, he would have had little or no inclination to provide anything approaching a conservative estimate of his benefactor's success. If anything, the case would have been quite the opposite.

That said, it does seem that the Ghaznavid armies enslaved an extraordinarily large number of Indians. Estimates found in the sources vary, although they are uniformly quite large. Referring back to their twelfth campaign, the sixteenth-century *Tarikh-i Alfi*, for example, suggests that the Ghaznavid armies enslaved some 750,000 people. Elsewhere, al-Utbi reports that, during the much earlier Ghaznavid invasion of Peshawar and Waihand in 1001, Mahmud and his troops captured some 100,000 youths. Written long after the actual event, the *Tarikh-i Firishta* reports that, following the Ghaznavid capture of Thanesar in 1014, 'the army of Islam brought to Ghazna about 200,000 captives and so much wealth, so that the capital appeared like an Indian city, no soldier of the camp being without wealth, or without many slaves'.[2]

It is difficult to know how much credence to give these accounts, many of which were written by chroniclers who were not present at the events described, or who lived centuries later and drew their information from oral tradition or other written sources whose reliability cannot be known. But focusing attention just on those sources whose authors were contemporaries of the events described, we find similar figures. For instance, in 1219–20, Minhaj al-Din Juzjani (1193–1265) fled from the Mongol armies in the wake of their invasion of his native Ghur, in central Afghanistan. He eventually sought refuge in Delhi where he found employment at the court of the Delhi Sultans, and it was there that he went to work crafting his universal history of the Islamic world, the *Tabaqat-i Nasiri*, which he completed in 1260.[3] According to Juzjani, the first ruler of the Shamsi slave dynasty, Qutb al-Din Aibak (r. 1206–10) reportedly enslaved some 20,000 individuals in Gujarat and another 50,000 at Kalinjar.[4] Turning to another contemporary source, we find similar figures presented in Zia al-Din Barani's *Tarikh-i Firuz Shahi*, a history of the Delhi Sultanate from the reign of the Shamsi ruler Ghiyath al-Din Balban (r. 1266–87) to the Tughluqid Firuz Shah (r. 1351–88). According to Barani, Sultan 'Ala' al-Din Khalji (r. 1296–1316) owned some 50,000 slave-boys and had another 70,000 working as construction labourers across his realm. Barani estimates that his own patron, Sultan Firuz Shah, owned some 180,000 slaves.[5]

Considering the figures mentioned in contemporary sources, it does seem plausible to conclude that the practice of enslaving captives occasionally resulted in the exportation of hundreds of thousands of individuals to markets beyond the Hindu Kush. While this practice increased during the Ghaznavid era, it must be emphasized that it neither began nor ended with them. The movement of Indian slaves to markets in the north and west also dates back to antiquity, long before the advent of Islam and longer still before the lifetime of Mahmud of Ghazna.

Yet there is a substantial amount of evidence that, throughout the medieval and early modern eras, Indian slaves were heavily trafficked to Central Asian markets. This can largely be attributed to specific policies regarding captives maintained during the long centuries of military expansion in India under the Ghaznavids, the Delhi Sultans and the Mughals. There are multiple explanations for why this might be the case. These include: the establishment of governmental structures under the Islamic dynasties that more closely bound India with other markets in the eastern Islamic world; the state-building efforts of the Ghaznavids and their successors who sought to expand their realms in South Asia; and, once those states were established, the tax revenue policies that they employed.

We find evidence regarding taxation policies in Barani's *Tarikh-i Firuz Shahi*. According to Barani, several Delhi Sultans adopted policies that involved the enslavement of individuals, or groups of individuals, who for a variety of reasons failed to satisfy their revenue assessments. Balban reportedly went so far as to order his military commanders to enslave anyone who remained resistant to his authority.[6] Barani notes that Sultan 'Ala' al-Din Khalji made it legal to enslave anyone who failed to pay their taxes. Later sources demonstrate that this policy remained in place even during the Mughal era.

The processes by which Indian slaves were exported to Central Asia appear to have continued, more or less unabated, throughout the Mughal era. Emperor Akbar reportedly tried to prohibit the enslavement of those Hindus defeated in war, but his efforts appear to have been only marginally successful, and were quickly forgotten during the reigns of his successors. As previously noted, Akbar himself reportedly ordered the capture and enslavement of many thousands of tribesmen who were guilty of obstructing caravan traffic en route to Qandahar. Further, during Akbar's reign, one Portuguese Jesuit, Father Antonio Monserrate, reported that the 'Gaccares' or Gakhar merchants, who dominated the Punjab region near the Salt Range, remained very active in exporting Indian slaves in exchange for Central Asian horses, the topic of the next chapter.[7] Several decades later, the Central Asian noble Abdullah Khan Firuz Jang, who served the

Mughals during the reigns of Jahangir (r. 1605–27) and Shah Jahan (r. 1628–58), encountered stiff resistance following his appointment to serve as the governor of Kalpi and Kher. In putting down the rebellion, he reportedly 'beheaded the leaders and enslaved their women, daughters and children, who were more than 2 lacks in number'.[8]

As was customary, these individuals would have been marched away from their family support systems to distant markets, including those on the far side of the Hindu Kush. Additionally, large numbers of people would have been driven into slavery having been sold by impoverished parents who, especially during periods of famine, would have preferred such an outcome to starvation. Over the centuries, groups of caravan traders including the Gakhars, Afghan Kuchis (or Powindas), and many others are known to have purchased such individuals and marched them through the mountain passes. They would then be exchanged for Central Asian horses, and other merchandise in demand in the subcontinent.

Indian Slaves in Central Asia

Indians were by no means the only slaves in Central Asian markets. Historical sources in the early modern era also refer to slave populations of other ethnic and religious

backgrounds, including Buddhist Mongols, Christian
Russians, Hazaras and other Afghans, and especially
Shia Iranians. But earlier Central Asian sources indicate
that a significant proportion of the Central Asian slave
population, and possibly even a majority, originated
in India.

Most of these slaves would have been purchased by
caravan traders and marched to Central Asian markets,
although there were other means by which they were
transported between regions. For instance, the Mughals
regularly included skilled slaves as gifts along with
ambassadorial exchanges. Indian merchants and other
travellers were also occasionally robbed and then sold
into slavery. Victorious armies were also known to
have enslaved defeated Mughal soldiers. To cite one
exceptional example, in 1646, Shah Jahan dispatched a
large army from Kabul to Balkh, which the Mughal forces
occupied. Shah Jahan then placed his son Aurangzeb in
charge of another army, with instructions to reinforce the
Mughal forces and prepare for the next objective, which
was to occupy the ancestral capital of Samarqand. But the
winter that year proved to be unusually long and severe,
with food becoming scarce and local support even more
so. Ultimately, the Mughal troops were forced to retreat.
According to the Central Asian chronicler, Muhammad
Yusuf Munshi, the Central Asian 'wolves' captured the

Indian 'slave-sheep' as they fled, and marched them to the slave markets of Samarqand, Tashkent and Turkestan, at the southern edge of the Central Asian steppe.[9] This apparently created such a surplus in the market that the price for slaves plummeted. While in 1589 a young and healthy male slave was sold in Samarqand for 225 tanga, in the wake of the Mughal retreat a slave could be had for only 84 tanga.

There is no precise measure by which we can definitively determine the exact number of Indian slaves in Central Asia at any given time, but available primary sources can be used to advance a rough estimate. One source in particular provides insight into a cross-section of the Central Asian slave population in late-sixteenth-century Samarqand. The *Majmu'a-i-watha'iq*, a judicial record belonging to a *qadi* in Samarqand with entries dating from 1588 to 1592, includes seventy-seven entries that pertain to either the manumission or the sale of slaves.[10] From this limited sample, we find that over 58 per cent of those slaves whose region of origin is mentioned were from India. It would be irresponsible to apply this figure to the whole of Central Asia during the early modern era. But this evidence does support our assertion that many of the tens and hundreds of thousands of individuals enslaved in India were sold in Central Asian markets.

Throughout the early modern era, slaves were abundant in Central Asia, and they were used for many purposes. The most famous were the *ghulams* (or, in Arabic, *mamluks*): elite military slaves whose remarkable skills and unwavering loyalty enabled them to rise to positions of command. But this population was comprised almost exclusively of Turks who had been either purchased or captured from the pastoral nomadic steppe. Military slaves represented a minority of the slave population even during the Samanid era, before the Ghaznavids had cast off their Persian overlords and established themselves as an independent power deep in the heart of Afghanistan.

By the early modern era, the day of the Central Asian military slave had long since passed. During this period, the majority of slaves in Central Asia were used not for military purposes, but primarily as household workers, manual labourers on construction projects, and agricultural labourers on the plantation-style farms of the Central Asian dynastic families. More specifically, large numbers of slaves were involved in planting and harvesting crops, tending to livestock, working in brick factories and digging irrigation canals. Skilled slaves were especially valuable and were therefore in high demand, although young women were, perhaps not surprisingly, in even greater demand. A seventeenth-century history of the Juybari Sheikhs in Bukhara records that one of these Sufi Sheikhs owned some 300 slaves, another owned 400, and a third owned 500 slaves, the majority of whom were used in making pottery, working as carpenters, and tending to the crops and livestock on his farms.[11] Such an arrangement appears to have been relatively common for Central Asia's ruling nobility and the wealthy. While our sources frequently refer to Indian slaves working alongside Russians, Persians, Mongols and others, large numbers of Indian slaves were clearly present throughout the entire sedentary zone, and, in smaller numbers, even among the nomads of the steppe.

The Central Asian slave trade remained active up to the end of the nineteenth century. Available figures for the total number of slaves in the region during the nineteenth century suggest that there were as many as 100,000 slaves in the Bukharan Amirate alone, with tens of thousands more in the Turkmen territories, and in the Khivan and Khoqand Khanates. But while the earlier evidence suggests that a substantial proportion, and perhaps even the majority, of the total Central Asian slave population originated in India, by this time, observers report that most of the slaves were Persian. This was a result of two factors: the drastic reduction in the availability of Indian slaves from the beginning of the eighteenth century on the one hand, and the corresponding rise of Turkmen slave-raids into the nearby Iranian settlements in the wake of Safavid military decline and imperial collapse on the other.

Within India, the end of the large-scale export of slaves seems to have stemmed from two causal factors. First, the supply of Indian slaves is likely to have diminished considerably following Aurangzeb's death in 1707 and the abrupt end of Mughal military expansion. In later years, British colonial expansion in India is known to have created its discontents, as well. But the policies enforced were different. The unfortunate individuals who were forced into bonded labour or indentured servitude under the British generally found themselves transported by ship to other parts of the British Empire, not marched by caravan to Central Asia. Second, unlike under the Delhi Sultans and the Mughals, in later years slaves seem to have been generally excluded from the taxation system.

The exportation of Indian slaves to Central Asian markets, a staple commodity in this trade from Ghaznavid times, seems to have come to an abrupt halt in the early eighteenth century. There is one notable exception to this trend that deserves mention. In the nineteenth century, members of an ethnic group known as 'Chitralis' began to appear in Central Asian slave markets. These were Hindus who came from Chitral, a region deep in the Karakoram mountains located to the east of Badakhshan. One reason for the sudden appearance of the Chitralis in the Bukharan slave markets is that, as the availability of Hindus from farther south diminished, Central Asian slave raiders turned to nearby Chitral. This trade was sufficiently profitable that Murad Beg, the ruler of Kunduz, in northern Afghanistan, required his subjects to pay their taxes in Chitrali and Hazara slaves, which he could then sell in the slave markets of Bukhara, Khoqand, or elsewhere.

Prior to turning to a discussion of the movement of Central Asian horses to Indian markets, one might ask what happened to all of the Indian slaves. Where did they go? The answer, of course, is that their descendants are still there. In 1832, on the eve of the First Anglo-Afghan War, the British agent Alexander Burnes (1805–41) was sent on a diplomatic mission to Bukhara. On his return, Burnes repeated the popular adage that, 'three fourths of the people of Bokhara are of slave extractions'.[12] That is not to say that a full 75 per cent of the city's population continued to be slaves. Rather, a great number of the people who lived in the Amirate had ancestors who at one time or another had been slaves. These slaves, Indians included, were eventually manumitted, or managed to earn money through extra labour to purchase their freedom. Once free, they were absorbed into the local population and lived out their lives in the region.

7. HORSES

These horses are exported to India [in droves], each one numbering six thousand or more or less . . . When they reach the land of Sind with their horses, they feed them with forage, because the vegetation of the land of Sind does not take the place of barley, and the greater part of the horses die or are stolen. They are taxed on them in the land of Sind [at the rate of] seven silver dinars a horse, at a place called Shahnaqar [Hashtnagar], and pay a further tax at Multan, the capital of the land of Sind . . . In spite of this, there remains a handsome profit for the traders in these horses, for they sell the cheapest of them in the land of India for a hundred silver dinars (the exchange value of which in Moroccan gold is twenty-five dinars), and often sell them for twice or three times as much. The good horses are worth five hundred [silver] dinars or more.[1]

—Ibn Battuta, c.1332

Our focus thus far has been on cotton textiles, slaves, and other Indian commodities that were transported in large quantities to Central Asian markets. At the same time, Multanis and other caravan traders supplied Indian markets with large amounts of Central Asia's legendary fruits, both fresh and dried. These included dozens of varieties of melons, apples, pears, pomegranates and grapes, as well as prunes, apricots and raisins. Other merchandise available in dried Central Asia and regularly exported to India included: fine silks, made in the region or imported from China or Persia; leather, wool and furs from the steppe; rubies and other precious stones; Chinese porcelain; several varieties of high quality paper produced in the region; and, of course, the exceptionally strong two-humped Bactrian camels, which could carry some 50 per cent more weight than the smaller Indian dromedaries and were better equipped to travel the frigid passes of the Hindu Kush.

These were not the only goods exchanged between India and Central Asia, but they were all commonly found packed on the backs of the pack animals or otherwise transported between regions. But of all the merchandise that moved from Central Asia to India, only the trade in horses was of sufficient magnitude that it could approach Central Asia's thirst for Indian textiles and slaves. For this reason, those same Multanis who moved wealth from India to Central Asia in the form of cotton textiles were also known to purchase herds of horses to move it back to India.

It remains unclear exactly when horses were first domesticated in the Inner Asian steppe, but it seems likely to have been sometime near the end of the third millennium BCE. Ancient authors, including Herodotus in the fifth century BCE, identify the Central Asian nomads as the principal breeders of horses, both for their own use and for trade with those in the sedentary world. The fact that the ancient Indian *ashvamedha*, or horse sacrifice, is described already in the Rig Veda indicates that Indians were involved in this exchange many centuries before Herodotus. The Puranas, the Mahabharata and other ancient Indian religious texts connect the horse trade with the Ashvakas, the 'horse folk' living beyond the north-west frontier of the subcontinent. As discussed below, the association of the Inner Asian steppe with the movement of large numbers of horses to India continued throughout the ages, lasting even into the twentieth century. In the novel *Kim* (1901), Rudyard Kipling crafted the character of Mahbub Ali as a British spy who posed as an Afghan horse trader so that he would be so ordinary as to not draw unwanted attention as he travelled from India, 'far and far into the Back of Beyond'.

Inner Asian pastoralists raised a variety of livestock, but in terms of their social and economic importance none could match the horse. Nomads bred horses in great numbers for transportation, hunting, warfare and trade, as well as consumption of horsemeat and milk. Nomads' leisure activities revolved around equestrian activities, which honed their combat skills. A nomadic clan's herd of horses could be very large, reaching even into the tens of thousands, and so the need to locate fresh pastureland dictated seasonal migration patterns. In virtually every way, horses represented an essential part of Inner Asian pastoral-nomadic life. Rather than chests full gold and silver, it was the size of the herd that was the measure of a clan's wealth.

Caravan traders and other people in the neighbouring sedentary civilizations on the Eurasian periphery, especially in China, but also India, Russia and the Middle East, valued camels as beasts of burden. But they found horses to be by far the most desirable commodity that Central Asians had to offer. Unlike pastoral-nomadic peoples, the sedentary peoples' demand for horses had little to do with dietary needs for protein and calorie intake. Sedentary peoples tended to prefer sheep, goats, chickens and pigs (the latter especially in China and Russia). But none of these animals could match the domesticated horse for speed in transportation, strength at pulling a cart or a plow, and especially for obedience in supporting cavalry on fast-moving military campaigns. Until the advent of the railroad and the motor car at the turn of the twentieth century, Eurasia's sedentary civilizations turned to the pastoral nomads of the vast Inner Asian steppe for horses.

Turning to early modern India, there were several factors that contributed to a sustained need to import large numbers of Inner Asian horses. The first of these stemmed from the increased importance that cavalry began to play in South Asian warfare from the early Ghaznavid era onwards. Throughout the medieval and early modern eras, north India's Turko-Afghan rulers profited from trade networks that stretched far to the north-west, and this gave them direct access to the horse trading communities in the vast Inner Asian breeding grounds. Indeed, one can argue that these states were able to rise to power when and where they did precisely because of their access to this critical military asset. Demand grew as horses became an increasingly important component of successful militaries, and the caravan traders who supplied Central Asian markets with Indian textiles and slaves returned with larger and larger numbers of horses through Afghanistan's mountain passes and pastures. Recall that, during the time of Akbar, the Gakhars of the Salt Range were widely known for trading Indian slaves for Central Asian horses.

Because of the advantages that horses provided in terms of speed and tactical agility, maintaining a large cavalry became a cornerstone of military strategy under the Delhi Sultans, Mughals, and their successor states. As one can imagine, once cavalry warfare was introduced it did not take long for rulers throughout the subcontinent to embrace these new cavalry-based techniques in order to defend themselves against the faster moving and superior forces of their Delhi Sultan opponents.

The rise in cavalry warfare among South Asian militaries led to an increased demand for horses. But efforts to breed horses within India were, with few exceptions, doomed to failure. The Dutch scholar, Jos Gommans, has studied this topic in considerable detail, and his conclusions merit attention.[2] According to Gommans, the critical factor that sustained this trade had to do with India's climatic conditions, which severely hindered efforts to breed a supply of horses in India. The long and hot summers together with abundant river networks, fertile soil and the annual monsoon rains were ideal for an expansive agrarian civilization. But these factors were not necessarily conducive to breeding horses. Put simply, horses failed to thrive in India's extreme heat. Further, unlike in Central Asia, in India arable land was a precious resource for farming, leaving little pastureland for horses to graze. Most of the land was too parched to grow anything, including grass, during the dry season. It was then flooded by the monsoons and used for growing crops. Even the small amount that was irrigated and set aside for horses still lacked Central Asia's nutritious alfalfa and broadleaf grasses that the animals needed.

Instead of a rich diet of vegetation or hay, Indian horses were fed a diet that could sustain the animals and maintain their outward appearance, but did not keep them healthy. This included grains, which were occasionally mixed with ghee or sugar in order to increase the calories and keep the animal from appearing emaciated. During his visit to Delhi, the seventeenth-century French traveller, linguist and botanist, Jean de Thévenot, reported that the Mughal stables included a large number of horses from Central Asia and Persia, as well as Arabians, the most beautiful of which were reserved for the Emperor himself. In describing how the horses were fed, he writes:

> They have neither oats nor barley given them in the Indies; so that foreign horses when they are brought thither can hardly feed. The way they treat them is thus: every horse has a groom, he curries and dresses him an hour before day, and so soon as it is day makes him drink; at seven of the clock in the morning, he gives him five or six balls of a composition called *donna*, made of three pounds of flower (flour), the weight of five *pechas* of butter, and of four *pechas* of *jagre*; these balls are at first forced down his throat, and so by degrees he is accustomed to that way of feeding, which in some months after he grows fond of.[3]

While such a diet could keep the animals alive, it was very unhealthy and, combined with the severe heat and insufficient exercise, Indian mares quickly became infertile. In the thirteenth century, Marco Polo observed that, although the rulers of Malabar imported some 10,000 horses each year, 'by the end of the year there shall not be one hundred of them remaining, for they all die off. And this arises from mismanagement, for those people do not know in the least how to treat a horse'.[4] Polo spoke with some authority, having spent an extended period of time among horses while working among the Mongols in China.

The horses that Polo referred to were very likely the 'Bahri' variety, bred principally in Khurasan and Central Asia, and then driven southward to the Persian Gulf where they were loaded onto ships and transported to Indian markets by sea (bahr). According to Polo, local consumers paid some 2.2 million dinars for the 10,000 horses that Malabar received every year. Nearly a century and a half later, in 1442, the Central Asian traveller 'Abd al Razzaq Samarqandi visited the Persian port of Hormuz, which he found to be a busy international entrepôt and an important horse market. A couple of decades later, in 1466, the Russian traveller Afanasi Nikitin was similarly impressed by the commercial stature of Hormuz when he travelled through that port on his way to the Bahmanid Sultanate in the Deccan. Echoing Marco Polo's observations, Nikin was shocked to find that, even though 'horses are not born in that country', so many were imported that the Bahmanid Sultan Muhammad III (r. 1463–82) could raise a cavalry force of half a million.[5] These were also Bahri horses, bred in Central Asia, Khurasan and Arabia and transported to Indian ports by sea.

These numbers are impressive, but the annual trade in Bahri horses was much smaller than the trade in 'Turki' horses, bred in the Qipchaq Steppe or Turkmen territories east of the Caspian Sea and then brought to Indian markets overland, through the Khyber and other passes. Turki horses were much shorter and stockier than the taller, elegant and more expensive Arabians. But Turki horses were in great demand because of their exceptional strength and stamina, and much lower price. For this reason, they constituted the overwhelming majority of the subcontinent's horse population. These were the horses that the famous fourteenth-century Tunisian traveller Ibn Battuta encountered as he passed through the Golden Horde, in southern Russia, and which he describes as being driven to India in herds of several thousand animals each, in the excerpt from his travel account that begins this chapter.

The profits from this trade were substantial, but so were the risks. According to Ibn Battuta, Indian consumers paid twenty-five times more for Turki horses than what the horse traders had paid for them in the steppe. While this may appear to be exorbitant, one must remember that horse traders suffered substantial losses due to illness, starvation and theft along the way, and their livestock would have been taxed, perhaps several times, en route to the Indian markets. Still, the sustained demand and substantial profits ensured a steady traffic in horses, which brought considerable income to mediatory states as well. Gommans suggests that the Indo-Afghan Durranis flourished in the eighteenth century at least partly by carving out a state along the trade routes connecting India with Central Asia, which enabled them to earn substantial profits by taxing the annual horse trade. Much the same could be said for the Afghan Suris, Lodis and others before them.

Indian demand for Central Asian horses remained steady throughout the Mughal era. During his time in Kabul, Babur observed a modest 7,000 to 10,000 horses being taken through that province en route to Indian markets each year.[6] Of course, that number did not include horses taken through the Bolan and other passes, or by the maritime routes by which traders also brought horses to Indian markets. It should be stressed that there was considerable variation in the rhythm of the trade, as demand would fluctuate dramatically if, for example, there were a sudden increase in military conflict in India. At the same time, the movement of horses could diminish due to political conflicts or other problems that obstructed traffic on the caravan routes. As large numbers of horses required large amounts of pasture, in particularly dry years horse traders may have been reluctant to risk their investment by moving their herds across wasteland, even if demand was substantial.

European observers who lived in India and worked in the Mughal court provide surprisingly large estimates of the magnitude of the overland Central Asian horse trade. Again, the figures they provide should be taken as impressionistic estimates and not factual numbers based on tax receipts, customs records or other documentary evidence. Nevertheless, the French traveller and physician to Emperor Aurangzeb, François Bernier, wrote in the latter part of the seventeenth century that some 25,000 Turki horses were brought annually from the Bukharan Khanate to India by overland routes, with more coming by other overland routes through Persia and also by sea.[7] At roughly the same time as Bernier, another seventeenth-century French traveller and jeweller, Jean-Baptiste Tavernier, ventured a much higher estimate. According to Tavernier, Central Asian caravan traders brought some 60,000 horses to Indian markets through Kabul each year.[8] This figure is repeated by Jean de Thévenot in his description of 'Caboul, or Caboulistan', which mentions that, although the region suffered from a harsh, cold and dry climate, 'nevertheless it is very rich, because it hath a very great trade with Tartary, the country of the Usbecs, Persia, and the Indies. The Usbecs alone sell yearly above threescore thousand (60,000) horses there'.[9] According to the Italian traveller and employee of the Mughal court, Niccolao Manucci (1639–1717), each year more than 100,000 horses were moved from the Bukharan Khanate to India, 12,000 of which were taken directly into Aurangzeb's stables.[10] Even as late as the 1770s, long after the decentralization of the Mughal Empire and well after the Battle of Plassey, another French traveller, Comte de Modave, reported that each year caravan traders supplied India with some 45,000 to 50,000 horses.[11]

Additional evidence lends some credence to these estimates. Focusing on the eighteenth century, Gommans estimates that there were, at any given time, between 400,000 and 800,000 horses in India. Considering infertility rates and death due to such causes as illness, poor health stemming from an improper diet, and physical trauma, he calculates that this entire population needed to be replaced every seven to ten years. Demand was certain to have increased during periods of greater military conflict. But even during sustained periods of relative peace there appears to have been a steady turnover in the horse population, which propelled a very large trade in Central Asian horses. Considering available figures regarding imports and their average prices, Gommans concludes that the total value of the annual horse trade should be placed at approximately 20 million rupees, or 'more than three times the total of Bengal exports to Europe by the English and Dutch East India Companies together'.[12]

In general, the Mughal and Uzbek states embraced policies designed to foster trans-regional trade, and their efforts generally met with success. Each year, caravan traders moved thousands of camel-loads of Indian textiles to Central Asian markets, as well as large numbers of Indian slaves. Our sources suggest that the number of individuals enslaved and exported to foreign markets was occasionally quite large, reaching even into the hundreds of thousands. But such instances were exceptional occurrences; one might argue that it was precisely *because* these instances were exceptional that the chroniclers mentioned them in their narratives. On average, it seems reasonable to suggest that the number of Indian slaves exported to Central Asia would have been in the area of several thousand people each year.

This chapter has demonstrated that Indian demand for horses represents another extraordinarily important aspect of India's commercial relationship with Central Asia, and one that was more consistent than the trade in slaves. Indians are known to have imported Central Asian horses already in antiquity, but the trade grew dramatically along with the rise in cavalry-based warfare during the medieval and early modern eras, and it lasted even into the twentieth century. In terms of its total value, the horse trade would have more than offset the trade in Indian slaves, and indeed it may very well constitute the single-most important aspect of the Indo-Central Asian commercial exchange.

Yet if we are to appreciate the full magnitude of India's commercial relationship with Central Asia, we must also consider all of the Central Asian fruit, silks, leather, wool and paper exported to India on the one hand, and the thousands of camel-loads of Indian textiles, dyes, spices, rice and other commodities on the other. Considering the commercial exchange as a whole, it seems more than likely that, throughout the early modern era, the balance of trade remained firmly in India's favour.

8. THE LIFE AND DEATH OF A DIASPORA

> *Wherever there is a bazaar Hindoos are a necessary part of the establishment! These people are found amongst the buyers and sellers in all of the cities of Central Asia, and constitute the bankers or money changers in all commercial communities there . . . They form an indispensable part of the population. All financial affairs are entrusted to their management.*[1]
>
> —General Josiah Harlan, 'Prince of Ghor', c.1840

Multan was a centre for Indian commercial interactions with Central Asia long before the 'Multanis' first made their way into the historical record, during the Delhi Sultanate era. We have seen that, from the middle of the sixteenth century, the Multanis not only mediated

India's vibrant trade with Central Asia, they established settlements in key locations beyond the Hindu Kush and laid the foundation for an extensive commercial network that would endure even into the twentieth century. A circulating population of tens of thousands of Multanis, and then Shikarpuris, moved merchandise, wealth and information between north-western India and distant markets of Afghanistan, Central Asia, Iran and Russia, eventually reaching even as far as Moscow and St Petersburg.

We have also surveyed the commercial system that the hundreds of Multani and Shikarpuri firms used to maintain this network. From their time as young apprentices, agents of these family firms were instructed in complicated legal codes, accounting techniques, various methods to calculate interest, and other skills that they would need to utilize the commercial technologies available to them and maximize their profit potential. The agents would then be loaned a large amount of capital, usually in the form of cotton textiles, before they would travel by caravan to a distant market.

On arriving at these markets, the agents would settle into a caravanserai, commonly one owned by other Indians associated with their family firm. As they gradually sold their merchandise, the agents would reinvest the cash retrieved in other profitable activities, most notably short-term, high-interest moneylending ventures. Following this model, agents could realize a 200 to 300 per cent annual increase in their total wealth. After several years—the Multanis' average tenure abroad was seven or eight years—the agents would return home and settle their accounts with their creditors, the principal partners of their family firms. This system offered sufficient flexibility for Indian firms to take measured risks, abandon deteriorating markets for better opportunities elsewhere, and safely move large amounts of capital across dangerous regions.

We have also seen that the Indian merchants provided a variety of commercial services that earned them their hosts' appreciation and protection. At the same time, their unfamiliar religious practices and shrewd business acumen provoked ire among their neighbours. Central Asians quite often disliked the Indians, who occasionally suffered as victims of crimes and even persecution. The most extreme example of animosity towards Indian merchants took place in Iran during the second quarter of the eighteenth century, first by the Ghilzai Afghans who occupied the Safavid capital of Isfahan, and then throughout the country during the brutal reign of Nadir Shah. After Nadir Shah's assassination in 1747, many Multani firms were positively inclined to accept the patronage of Ahmad Shah Durrani, and relocate to the safe haven of Shikarpur, in Sind. From the late eighteenth century, Shikarpuris replaced Multanis as the dominant Indian commercial community in both Afghanistan and Central Asia.

We now direct attention to the Indian merchants' Eurasian network itself, examining its magnificent expanse and a number of the more important ways that it changed over time. In the long history of the Indian communities in Central Asia, there were considerable variations in the conditions under which they lived. Regardless, Indian merchants remained active in Central Asia even throughout the Russian Imperial era (1865–1918). However, already during the 1870s the Russian colonial administration implemented a series of policies designed to undermine the Indians' business interests in Central Asia. By the time of the Bolshevik Revolution, the once great network of thousands of merchants linking Indian markets with those in Central Asia had dwindled to just a handful of individuals.

A Eurasian Network

Each year, several thousand agents of Indian family firms left behind their wives and children in Multan, and then Shikarpur, and travelled by caravan to distant Eurasian locations where they would spend years of their lives.

The merchants favoured locations that offered the best opportunities for conducting trans-regional trade, or other lucrative ventures. Cities such as Kabul, Qandahar, Bukhara, Bandar Abbas, Isfahan and Astrakhan were home to Indian populations that ranged from a few hundred individuals to more than ten thousand in Isfahan. Indian traders also maintained sizeable communities in dozens of somewhat smaller regional cities across Afghanistan, Central Asia, Iran, and up the Caucasus into Russia, and they could be found in countless villages spread across the countryside as well. Of course, the population figures for Indian merchants inhabiting specific locations fluctuated, occasionally abruptly. Nevertheless, taking all of these communities into account, a figure of 35,000 seems a conservative estimate for the number of Indian agents of these family firms spread across Afghanistan, Central Asia, Iran and Russia at any given time between the seventeenth and twentieth century. As one might expect, there were a number of important transitions that these communities experienced during the more than three centuries of their existence.

Afghanistan

Throughout the early modern era, and even until the partition of India in 1947, Multani and Shikarpuri merchants were present in virtually all of the cities and villages of Afghanistan. Because of its substantial population, political stature and location along the most important of the trade routes connecting India with Central Asia, Kabul was the principal centre for Indian commercial activity in Afghanistan. The dominant role of Hindu merchants in Kabul was well established already in the 1620s, when the English diplomat Thomas Herbert reported that 'Bannians' constituted the majority of the city's population and that, other than two 'castles', caravanserais represented the most significant structures in the city.[2] Several decades later, in the 1660s, Thévenot also observed a substantial population of Hindu 'Banians' in the district of 'Caboulistan'. He noted that their 'chief charity' was contributing to the region's commercial infrastructure, specifically by digging wells and maintaining rest stops along the trade routes 'for the convenience of travellers'.[3] The position of Indian merchants in Kabul continued over the years. In the 1830s, Alexander Burnes also found that some eight 'great houses of agency' (Shikarpuri firms) had three hundred subsidiary families stationed in Kabul, and they dominated the region's trade.[4]

Other centres of Indian commercial activity in Afghanistan included Qandahar, another major political centre located on important trade routes connecting

India with Persia. In Qandahar, a substantial population of Hindu merchants resided in their own quarter of the city well into the twentieth century. In Herat, near the end of the eighteenth century, George Forster encountered one hundred Multanis who occupied two caravanserais and profited by conducting 'a brisk commerce and extending a long chain of credit'.[5] Other observations suggest that the size of the Indian population in Herat fluctuated considerably. While some reports give more modest figures, in 1810, just a few years after Forster passed through the city, the British Captain Charles Christie was surprised to find some six hundred 'highly respected' Hindu merchants in Herat representing a dominant commercial presence in the region.[6] In 1845, the French traveller Joseph-Pierre Ferrier passed through the city and reported that the Shikarpuri community there was exceptionally influential. He observed: 'The commerce of India with this city may be said to be almost entirely in their hands; they are held in great estimation by Yar Mohamed, and farm nearly all the taxes'.[7]

Herat was not the only location in Afghanistan where Shikarpuris worked within the government. Shikarpuris are known to have been deeply involved in the Durrani financial administration during the reign of Timur Shah (r. 1773–93), Ahmad Shah's son and successor.

They commonly purchased the right to serve as tax farmers, and also issued loans to government officials in order to fund military campaigns and other activities, both official and unofficial. Further, Hindu merchants served the Afghan state by collecting customs duties. One individual, whom the British agents Moorcroft and Trebek identify as Atma Ram, paid 25,000 rupees each year for the right to tax commercial traffic moving between Kabul and Bukhara.[8] Hindus remained active in the governing administration even during the reign of the 'Iron Amir', 'Abd al-Rahman Khan (r. 1890–1901), who strove to improve Afghanistan's trade with India by establishing an oversight board consisting of seven influential merchants: four Muslims and three Hindus. The Hindus are identified by name as Diwan Ishir Das, Yajal Das and Diwan Ramchand Shikarpuri.[9]

Looking back, we find that Indian moneylenders were ubiquitous in Durrani Afghanistan. In the early nineteenth century, Elphinstone reported that 'the Hindoos . . . are to be found over the whole kingdome of Caubul. In towns they are in considerable numbers as brokers, merchants, bankers, goldsmiths, sellers of grain, &c. There is scarce a village in the country without a family or two who exercise the above trades, and act as accountants, moneychangers, &c'.[10] Henry Pottinger, who travelled through Afghanistan in the early nineteenth century, also observed Hindu merchants operating in towns of all sizes, from regional capitals to the smallest villages.[11] To mention a few of these locations, Pottinger and others identify Hindu merchants in: Khojar, a small town where Multanis and Shikarpuris dominated the commercial economy to such an extent that every night the keys to the town were entrusted to the senior Brahmin; Haibak, a small town near Samangan on a trade route leading to Khulum; Bela; Tuman; Faizabad; Taliqan; Khanabad; Jalalabad; Maimana; Ghazni; Kafir Qil'a, the name of which translates as 'Fortress of the Infidel'; Tashkurgan (Khulum), located two days east of Balkh; Balkh itself; and, in the nineteenth century, Mazar-i Sharif. The full list of regional towns and villages of every size throughout Afghanistan where Multanis, Shikarpuris and other Indian merchants are documented to have resided and dominated trans-regional trade and various other aspects of the regional economy is simply too long to detail.

Central Asia

Much like in Afghanistan, Indian merchant communities in Central Asia could be found in virtually every major urban centre and regional town, and throughout much of the countryside as well. The earliest communities were established in Bukhara, Samarqand and Tashkent in the sixteenth century, and probably elsewhere, although direct evidence for other communities at that time is lacking. The sixteenth-century expansion of Multani communities across the region is supported by the tradition of a Hindu merchant community at Yangi Ariq, near Balkh, that their ancestors were encouraged to settle there during the reign of Abdullah Khan (r. 1583–98). Later, in the seventeenth century, the aforementioned Bukharan *farman* identifies Indian merchants throughout the region, specifically listing: 'Bukhara, Balkh, Badakhshan, Qunduz, Taliqan, Aibek, Ghuri, Baghlan, Shabarghan, Termiz, Samarqand, Nasaf (Qarshi) and Shahrisabz'.[12] The subsequent inclusion of the phrase 'and wherever else they may live' indicates that this was not meant to be an exhaustive list.

Indian Merchants in Their Bukharan Caravanserai (1890s)

Bukhara, not surprisingly, appears to have hosted the largest of the Indian communities in Central Asia. Mohan Lal observed that within the city itself there were a number of large caravanserais, and that 'most of them are inhabited by Hindu merchants'.[13] Working in the records of the Office of the Bukharan Khushbegi, the late Russian scholar G.L. Dmitriev found that Hindu merchants inhabited no fewer than nine caravanserais in nineteenth-century Bukhara, and he lists them by name: Alimjan, Abdullajan, Ibrahimjan, Serai-i Kalan, Serai-i Poi Astan, Amir, Tamaku, Karshi and Filkhana.[14] His sources also mention Indians inhabiting caravanserais in Samarqand, Tashkent, Andijan, Khoqand, Khojent, Kitab, Kulab, Khatirchi, Chimkent and Urateppe. Towards the end of the nineteenth century, the Central Asian novelist and reformer, Sadr al-Din 'Aini, wrote in his memoires that he recalled three specifically Indian caravanserais in Bukhara, each of which was home to some 150 Hindu moneylenders.[15] This estimate is corroborated by Arminius Vámbéry, who, in 1863, suggested that Bukhara was home to some 500 Indian merchants.[16]

Echoing Josiah Harlan's assertion at the beginning of this chapter, Vámbéry also observed that Hindu merchants were present throughout the region, in both urban and rural markets. Astonished to find them so widespread, he declared that, in the Bukharan Amirate, Hindu merchants had 'in some wonderful manner got all the management of money into their hands, there being no market, not even a village, where the Hindoo is not ready to act as usurer'.[17] Several decades later, at the turn of the century, the Danish geographer, Ole Olufsen observed that the Hindus' commercial interests had suffered severely under the Russian colonial administration—a topic we will address below—but in Bukharan territory they continued to dominate the moneylending industry in both the cities and villages.[18]

One trend in the gradual expansion of Indian commercial activity across the region merits particular attention. Analysing the evidence from the sixteenth and seventeenth centuries, we find references to Indian merchant communities across nearly the entire Bukharan state, excepting the Ferghana Valley. By the time the Russians invaded Ferghana in the 1860s, however, Indian merchants had become as ubiquitous there as everywhere else in the region. Russian colonial records pertaining to the Ferghana *oblast* (district) document Indian merchant communities in such major cities as Khoqand, Andijan, Osh, Namangan, Old Margilan, Skobelev (Ferghana City) and Chust, as well as in small cities and villages, including Rishtan, Yengi Kurgan, Ichkurgan, Kuba, Aul, Bulakoshi, Khojevat,

Chimion, Khoqan and Kishlak. While it remains conjecture, it is likely that the rise of the Khanate of Khoqand (1799–1876) and the state's achievements at expanding irrigation agriculture in the Valley increased commercial opportunities and drew hundreds more Indians into the region over the course of the late eighteenth and nineteenth centuries.

As was the case with Afghanistan, our sources refer to dozens of Indian communities in far too many Central Asian cities and villages to list here. In addition to the Bukharan Amirate, Russian colonial records place them in every *oblast* of Central Asia under Russian control, stretching even beyond the boundaries of modern Uzbekistan into the territories of modern Tajikistan, Kyrgyzstan and Kazakhstan (although citing the government's parasitic policies towards foreign merchants, they were conspicuously absent from of the Khivan Khanate). This leads us to estimate that, from the seventeenth century until the Indian communities began to diminish in size in the late nineteenth century, at any given time some 8,000 Indian merchants inhabited cities and villages across Central Asia.

In addition to this, during the nineteenth century, a smaller group of Shikarpuris, probably never more than 500, ventured northwards through Kashmir to take up residence in Kashgar, Yarkand and other cities and villages of Xinjiang, China. These Shikarpuris were engaged in the same commercial activities there as in other places, and they remained active in the region until the National Revolutionary Army defeated the Xinjiang provincial government at the Battle of Urumqi in 1933.

Iran

At the same time that the Multanis were becoming established in Bukhara, they were also extending their activities into Iran. They did this through the overland routes passing through Qandahar, as well as the maritime routes leading to the busy Persian Gulf port city of Bandar Abbas, the composition of which the seventeenth-century French traveller Jean Chardin estimated to be two-thirds Indian.[19] Still searching for an overland route by which the English could access the Indian Ocean trade, in 1562 Anthony Jenkinson made his way through Russia to Iran and encountered a community of Indian merchants in Qazvin, the Safavid capital at that time.[20] A few years later, two other English travellers, Thomas Bannister and Jeffrey Ducket, also journeyed through Russia on their way to Iran. They passed through Astrakhan, at the mouth of the Volga, and other locations known to host Indian communities in later years, but their account says nothing of an encounter with Indian merchants until they reached Kashan, which they described as an extraordinarily active commercial centre 'greatly frequented by the merchauntes of India'.[21]

We have observed above that, sometime after the Safavids moved their capital to Isfahan at the very end of the sixteenth century, that city became home to what was by far the largest Multani community outside of India. The Italian traveller Pietro Della Valle's 1617 account contains the earliest mention of Indians in Isfahan. Although he did not estimate the size of the community, his account does state that at that time Indians were already the most important of the foreign merchant communities in Safavid territories.[22] Twenty years later, Adam Olearius reported that Isfahan was home to 12,000 Indians, an astounding number corroborated by multiple accounts of a few decades later that present figures ranging between 10,000 and 15,000.[23]

Echoing reports of Hindu merchants in Central Asia, in 1660, Raphaël du Mans identified Multanis as ubiquitous and the principal textile brokers in Iran. In the 1670s, the English physician, John Fryer, reported that Indian merchants were present 'in all the cities of Persia'.[24] In general, this lends credence to Jean Chardin's assertion that, in the 1660s, Iran was home to more than 20,000 Multanis.[25] It seems likely that this figure remained more or less constant until the Ghilzai Afghan invasion in 1722.

Indian merchants had good reason to select Isfahan as a centre for their activities in the region. In addition to the proximity to their Safavid patrons, large caravans of thousands of camels loaded with Indian textiles regularly passed from India into Iran, and because of its location along the heavily trafficked trade routes, much of this made its way to Isfahan. Seventeenth-century Dutch observers estimated that caravans brought some 25,000 to 30,000 camel-loads of Indian textiles into Iran each year.[26] From Iran, Multanis could sell their merchandise locally or arrange to send it westwards to the Mediterranean, or northwards along the trade routes traversing the Caucasus and the Caspian Sea to markets in Russia and Eastern Europe.

Over the course of the seventeenth century, this northwards trade grew to become substantial, and it added commercial value to the northern Iranian provinces of Gilan and Shirwan. Indian communities began settling in these places shortly after the Safavids reclaimed them from the Ottomans at the beginning of the seventeenth century. They also settled in Mazandaran, on the southern shores of the Caspian Sea; in Tabriz, Baku and Ardabil in Azerbaijan; and in

Derbent, Terek, and many of the other smaller trading towns in the Caucasus.

Following the devastation they suffered in the second quarter of the eighteenth century, political authority in Iran began to normalize in the hands of the Zand and then the Qajar dynasties, and Indians returned in large numbers. By the end of the eighteenth century, Indians were again present in cities and villages across the country. The greatest density of Indian activity in Iran during this period seems to have been near the Persian Gulf. Edward Waring visited the city of Bushehr in 1802, and reported that, in that town, 'the Hindoos live unmolested by the Persians, and are neither insulted nor oppressed by the government'.[27] Farther to the north, in Baku, another traveller to the region observed in 1824 that, although 'Nadir Shah treated their predecessors with great cruelty; impaling them, and putting them to several kinds of tortures', Indians had no present complaints about their treatment.[28] As was the case in Afghanistan, towards the end of the nineteenth century George Curzon observed that Shikarpuris and other merchants from Sind had not only become the dominant merchants in Bushehr, Bandar Abbas, and other major trading cities and villages near the Persian Gulf, they regularly purchased the right to farm the taxes and gather customs in those places.[29]

Russia

In the 1630s, Multanis in Safavid Iran gradually began to direct their attention northwards, to market opportunities in Russia. Firms that were well established in Isfahan began sending agents to Gilan and Shirwan on the Caspian coastline, and then to Baku, in Azerbaijan. From Baku, the Multanis ventured further on to the Russian port city of Astrakhan, where Russian authorities granted them permission to establish a community that would eventually grow to more than two hundred merchants. As was the case for other foreign merchants communities, including Bukharans, Iranians and Armenians, the Indians in Astrakhan were assigned to their own *dvor*, technically a merchant courtyard, which in form and function served as a Russian caravanserai. This represented the central location for Indian commercial interaction with Russia until the middle of the eighteenth century, when Indians would redirect their trade to overland routes passing through Orenburg, a newly established Russian outpost in the steppe.

Because a substantial collection of Russian archival records relating to the activities of Indian merchants in Astrakhan were preserved and published, and then published again in an abridged English translation, a fair amount is known about Indian merchant activities in

Russia.[30] By and large, Indians' commercial portfolios in Russia were the same as they were in Bukhara, Isfahan and elsewhere. Alongside importing textiles, Indians in Russia engaged in a wide variety of moneylending ventures. While the number of Indians in Russia was smaller than elsewhere, the Russian records provide valuable insights into their extensive commercial activities. These records reveal that Indians in Astrakhan and its environs commonly accepted physical property as collateral for the loans they advanced. Over time, as some lenders defaulted on their payments, Indians became owners of a substantial amount of 'immovable property', which included homes, farms and shops. We also find that the Russian government occasionally imposed restrictions that limited the ability of Indians to travel beyond Astrakhan.

When they were not permitted to leave Astrakhan, the Indians arranged partnerships with Armenians and local merchants who could work on their behalf. When they were permitted, Indian merchants travelled and engaged in ventures across the Russian countryside. Archival records refer to an Indian presence in the Siberian commercial town of Krasnoyarsk, for example, and they also travelled up the Volga River to Tsaritsyn, Saratov, Kazan and Nizhny Novgorod. In 1679, a small group of Indians made their way to Moscow, where they were granted permission to stay. Five years later, their number had grown to twenty-one. Indians would later reach as far as St Petersburg, although even that was by no means the limit of their ambitions. In 1723, one Indian merchant, identified in the Russian records as Anburam Mulin, applied to Tsar Peter the Great (r. 1682–1725) for permission to travel to Arckangelsk on the White Sea in order to extend Indian commercial activities westwards to Germany, and to China in the east.[31]

Though the number of Indians at any given time in Russia was not great and their mobility was occasionally restricted, they were, nevertheless, substantial import-export agents. In 1722, one observer reported that the Armenians were doing quite well in Astrakhan, but 'the Banyans without doubt contribute most to its flourishing condition'.[32] Two years later, as the Ghilzai Afghans were destroying the Indians' commercial network in Iran, Russian records indicate that the Indians still brought to Astrakhan merchandise worth nearly 100,000 rubles—more than twice the value of the merchandise that Russian merchants brought.[33] The Indians remained active in Astrakhan even into the nineteenth century, although only in small numbers. By the middle of the eighteenth century, the larger part of their commercial interests in Russia had shifted eastwards, to an overland route leading through Central Asia.

This shift was a direct result of Russian colonial expansion into the region. During the first half of the eighteenth century, Russia gradually established a series of fortresses across the southern Siberian steppe. In addition to serving as military outposts for the protection of Russian territorial acquisitions against the Kazakhs and other Central Asian nomadic tribes, these fortresses also served as militarized commercial outposts, drawing merchants from across the region. This would eventually become known as the Orenburg Line, after the fortress by that name.

In 1735, the newly established Orenburg Dispatch Department began efforts to convince the Indians of Astrakhan to redirect their trade eastwards, away from the Caspian Sea. Considering the difficulties they were experiencing in Iran at the time, the Indians were rather easily convinced. Russian archival records indicate that the leader of Astrakhan's Marwari community, identified as Marwari Baraev, suggested to the Russian authorities that, if the steppe route from Bukhara were safe for travel, the Russians could expect some 600 Indian merchants at the commercial fair held at Orenburg each year.[34] By the time of Nadir Shah's death in 1747, Russian census figures show that the population of Indians in Astrakhan had dwindled from more than 200, to only fifty-one individuals.

Meanwhile, Orenburg increased dramatically as a place of commercial importance. One report from the Orenburg archives indicates that, in 1745, the annual Orenburg fair drew a substantial number of traders from both Bukhara and India, and that the Indians alone brought merchandise worth some 300,000 rubles. Orenburg was not alone: fairs at Troisk and other Russian outposts on the Orenburg Line similarly drew merchants from as far away as India, and archival records reveal that the Russians listed prices both in local currency and in rupees. Later, in the 1770s, a French traveller in India encountered some 300 Gujarati merchant families who were making their way northwards, to Orenburg.[35]

The magnitude of the overland caravan trade through Orenburg grew substantially greater during the late eighteenth and nineteenth centuries, alongside a corresponding increase in Russian commercial interests in Central Asian trade. In 1813, Mir Izzat Ullah, an Indian traveller to Central Asia, estimated that every year between 4,000 and 5,000 camels made their way from Bukhara to Russian trading outposts in the steppe. Whether it was Indian merchants or Bukharan merchants who owned them, the camels were reported to have been loaded principally with cotton textiles.[36] Indeed, several observers from this period indicate that cotton textiles were Russia's principal import from Bukhara well into the nineteenth century. The fact that Bukharan markets were largely dependent upon India for this commodity (see chapter four) suggests that, even if the observers were unaware of it, they were in fact reporting on an Indo-Russian transit trade through Central Asia.

Russian Colonial Policies in Central Asia, and the End of an Era

The Russian army conquered Tashkent in June 1865, and within a year it became apparent that the Russian administration had adopted a view on Indian merchant activities in the region that was markedly different from their predecessors. Already in April 1866, several months before Tashkent was even officially incorporated into the Russian Empire, Tsar Alexander II (r. 1855–81) signed a decree that both put a cap on the interest rates Indians could charge in Russian territory, and required the Indians to notarize all loan agreements in Russian courts. Our sources indicate that, for the next eleven years, Shikarpuris, Marwaris and other Indians continued to thrive in Russian colonial Central Asia, largely by circumventing these restrictions.

Considering that the Indians were British subjects living within the Russian Empire at the height of the

Great Game, one might have expected that the Russians would object to their presence based on concerns of national security. It seems reasonable to suggest that fears that Indian merchants could potentially serve as British spies may have driven the actions of some Russian colonial administrators. But Russian policies regarding the Indian merchants in their realm were crafted in response to an entirely different set of issues. From the outset, the Russian colonial administration determined that the Indians' moneylending activities were contrary to the best interest of the agricultural economy of the region. In particular, the Russians were concerned that Indian moneylenders were foreclosing on a large number of plots of land that had been used as collateral on defaulted loans. To the Russians, much more pressing than whether or not the Indians were informing the British of Russian activities in the region (they were) was that the Indians were gradually taking ownership of vast stretches of the region and transforming local farmers into a class of landless labourers.

In the meantime, Russian control over Turkestan expanded rapidly. In 1868, the newly appointed governor general of the Turkestan Krai, Konstantin von Kaufman (1867–86), launched a successful campaign against Bukhara, reducing the Amirate to a protectorate and annexing Samarqand. In the same year, the Russians reduced the Khoqand Khanate to a protectorate as well. Khoqand remained in a state of crisis until the Russians finally extinguished the Khanate in 1876 and established the Ferghana Oblast in its place. In 1873, the Khivan Khanate was similarly reduced to a protectorate.

As the Russians consolidated their control throughout the region, it became clear to Kaufman's administration that the 1866 decree restricting Indians' moneylending activities was insufficient to achieve its goals. In June 1877, Kaufman began to consider other methods. After a series of official exchanges, he reached a consensus with his generals that the transfer of agricultural land and other immovable property to Indians should be prohibited.[37]

But enforcing restrictions on the Indians' moneylending operations proved to be more complicated than simply issuing a decree. For centuries, the Indians had been deeply involved in Central Asian agricultural production. The Indians operated a rural credit system throughout the region, and farmers depended on them for loans in the spring planting season. There were local moneylenders who tried to compete with the Indians, but the Russians found them to be too undercapitalized to be effective. Kaufman was genuinely concerned that if he should act too hastily in restricting the Indians' activities, his efforts may cause a region-wide famine.

In the end, the Russians resolved to apply a two-part solution that involved restricting Indians' moneylending activities while simultaneously providing Central Asian farmers with an alternate source of credit. Kaufman's Chief of the Office, P. Kablukov, advocated for establishing a series of state credit offices throughout the region that would effectively undermine the Indians by providing a more affordable alternative. Kaufman agreed and on 7 November 1877 he issued a new directive, Circular No. 8560, which he declared would 'fence off the population of the region under my rule from the Indians' exploitation'.[38] He submitted the following to Tsar Alexander's Military Minister for approval, which, when granted, gave the Circular the force of law.

Extract from Circular No. 8560

1. From this time Indians are forbidden to buy, or otherwise receive according to any contracts and penalties, land property, even for temporary usage.
2. Any land property which Indians received by will, gift, or other means, must be sold within six months.

3. Indians are forbidden to take land on pawn and lease.

4. The auctioning of the immovable property of the indigenous population based on documents of the Indians is forbidden, even if such documents are based on immovable property. It is forbidden even to look at or discuss these papers.

5. Instead of such selling of immovable property, the money owed to the Indians will be paid, with the assistance of policemen or other officials, from the profit, which the debtors earn from their immovable property. This will amount to not more than one-third of the debtor's annual profit from this immovable property, as stated in paragraph 653 of the Promissory Note Rule.

6. The personal arrest of the indigenous debtors, prior to their payment of their debt, is disallowed.

7. The following moveable property may not be sold or auctioned, provided the person has not overindulged in it: daily clothing, furniture, agricultural tools, items necessary for life, domestic and work livestock.

The Indians quickly found themselves in dire straits. As we have seen, the Indian commercial system involved importing a substantial amount of Indian merchandise, principally textiles, which had been loaned to them by the directors of their firms. As they sold their merchandise, the Indians then used the proceeds as capital to begin extending interest-earning loans. Rather than amassing wealth in cash, they deliberately worked to keep it invested in a variety of ventures throughout the region. But as word spread about the nature of Circular No. 8560, debtors stopped making payments on their loans, and the restrictions left the Indians with no recourse to recover their capital. This left the Indian agents impoverished, and unable to repay their own creditors, the directors of their family firms at home. Indian merchants issued desperate appeals pleading with Kaufman to reconsider these restrictions, and many threatened to withdraw from the region completely. On the bottom of one such appeal, Kaufman wrote that the Indians' request should be 'left without any attention'.[39]

Kaufman did eventually give some attention to the Indians' plight. While working to undermine Indian moneylending business, Kaufman recognized that his subjects stood to benefit from the Indians' other commercial interests in the region. This brought him into conflict with several of his own subordinate governors who had been overly enthusiastic in their appropriation of Indians' property. After some debate, Kaufman ordered that Indians would be forbidden from owning agricultural land, but that they would be permitted to retain ownership of the many caravanserais, houses, and shops that they owned and which were critical to the continuation of their trans-regional trade interests in the region.

Predictably, such a gesture was insufficient to convince most Indians to remain in the region. Kablukov's proposal for a new state banking system was approved in 1879, and two years later Kaufman opened the new Central Asian Commercial Bank with half a million rubles in capital. The banking network spread through the region. Denied the proceeds from their moneylending ventures and frustrated by legal obstacles that kept them from retrieving even the principal that they had advanced as loans prior to the publication of Kaufman's Circular, the number of Indian merchants in Russian Central Asia quickly diminished.

Travelling through the Ferghana Valley in the 1880s, Henry Lansdell observed only some thirty Hindus remaining in Khoqand. Dodging the Bolshevik authorities in 1918, the British Lieutenant Colonel Frederick Bailey encountered a small community of Hindus farther to the east, in Andijan. This remnant of a great merchant network appealed to Bailey for help in moving their wealth, which amounted to some two million rubles, safely to India.[40] After centuries of trading and amassing fortunes in the region, in these decades the Indians' urgent financial concerns focused on the need to liquidate their property and devise a safe way to move their wealth to India.

Shikarpuris and other Indian merchants remained active in Bukhara even after the turn of the century, although there too their numbers had diminished. When Colonel Bailey passed through Bukhara in 1919, he encountered a small community of only twenty-five Shikarpuris. There were more dispersed in other urban and rural areas throughout the Amirate, but these too would eventually trickle back across Afghanistan. In 1926, the USSR general census reported that the thirty-seven Indians who remained in Soviet Central Asia were officially registered as permanent citizens. Later reports indicate that many of them eventually made their way back home.[41]

9. CONCLUSION

The caravan trade linking Indian markets with those in Central Asia stretches back to antiquity, and continued even into the modern era. Taking issue with notions that Central Asia had become more isolated from its neighbours in the early modern era, this volume has sought to demonstrate that, at least in terms of its commercial relations with India, the situation was quite the opposite. With only periodic disruptions, the Bukharan Khanate and Mughal Empire, and their successors, made a sustained effort to encourage trans-regional commerce between their regions. These states invested heavily in developing a commercial infrastructure that would facilitate the caravan trade, welcomed foreign merchants to their realms, and offered them protection and a predictable commercial environment in which to conduct their trade.

These efforts bore fruit. Each year caravans left India with many thousands of camels loaded principally with Indian textiles, as well as dyes, spices, rice and other grains, raw and refined sugar, precious stones, weapons and, from the early nineteenth century, tea. Large numbers of enslaved Indians were forced to march alongside these caravans on their way to slave markets in Central Asia, never to return. In exchange, Central Asian caravan traders sent to India tens of thousands of Turki horses per year, as well as large amounts of the fruit for which the region was famous, Central Asian silks and paper. Central Asian merchants also orchestrated a substantial transit trade in Chinese porcelains and textiles, Inner Asian leather goods, Siberian furs and other merchandise produced in the steppe, as well as precious metals.

India's caravan trade with Central Asia was considerable, and it was no simple peddler trade. We have seen that, throughout the early modern era, merchants did much more than buy goods cheaply in one market in order to transport them to another market and sell them for a profit, only to do the same on their return journey. Powinda nomads were the principal carriers of the merchandise, annually leading their caravans from their summer destinations of Bukhara, Samarqand and other Central Asian locations far into India, reaching Bengal and the Deccan in the winter. But it was the Multani and Shikarpuri firms and their legions of agents who were the driving force that propelled India's trade with Central Asia.

During the Delhi Sultanate period, Multani firms had earned a reputation as large-scale financiers heavily involved in India's textile trade with foreign markets. In the fourteenth and fifteenth centuries, they gradually developed an expansive network across much of north and north-west India. From the sixteenth century, an increasing number of European maritime traders made their way to the region, injecting large amounts of silver into the Indian economy in exchange for Indian spices, textiles and other merchandise. This led to increasingly competitive market conditions in India and, combined with improved political relationships among the Mughals and their Uzbek and Safavid neighbours, the Multanis recognized an opportunity. From the middle of the sixteenth century, Multanis began to establish semi-permanent communities in a handful of locations conducive to mediating trade with markets beyond India's north-west frontier. In the seventeenth century, the number of Multani agents in Uzbek Central Asia and Safavid Iran reached into the tens of thousands, and the magnitude of their trade increased as well. Observers identified the Multanis as the most important foreign traders in both regions, and the premier dealers in cotton textiles.

The Multanis and, from the late eighteenth century, Shikarpuris, orchestrated an extensively integrated commercial system that connected north-west India with distant markets beyond the boundaries of the subcontinent. The great family firms were deeply invested in the production of cotton textiles in India, and they exploited those interests to the benefit of the agents whom they would send to Central Asia, or other far-flung locations. Rather than cash, the Multani and Shikarpuri firm directors loaned their agents large amount of cotton textiles. The agents travelled by caravan to their assigned markets and, once there, they gradually began to exchange their cloth for cash.

As they conducted their trade the Indians did not simply save up their money for their return journey, nor did they immediately use it to purchase locally produced merchandise that enjoyed a high demand in South Asian markets. Rather, they were trained to put their wealth to work by extending a variety of types of loans, including short-term high interest loans in urban settings and loans to finance agricultural production across the Central Asian countryside. The latter activity involved extending loans to farmers at planting time in exchange for a percentage of the harvest, and commonly purchasing the remainder of the harvest for cash. They were also known to use their capital resources to purchase the right to farm taxes, and even collect customs duties. These services were greatly valued by their hosts and, along with their trans-regional trade connections, explains why the Bukharans, Safavids, Durranis and others were keen to welcome large numbers of Hindu merchants into their realms and offer them the state's protection.

In terms of explaining the Indians' success, it is important to note that Muslim merchants in Central Asia, as in other regions of the Islamic world, were well known for using a number of legal devices to circumvent the Quranic prohibition of *riba*, extending loans for interest. That is to say, the Indians had no monopoly on moneylending in Central Asia. Rather, they excelled in this trade primarily because they had access to greater amounts of capital than their local competitors and they were exceptionally skilled at managing risk. This equipped them with an advantage over local competition, and in Central Asia they exercised that advantage even into the twentieth century.

Russian colonial expansion into Central Asia brought about the end of the Indian merchant network. Within months after the Russian conquest of Tashkent in 1865, the administration began to implement a series of policies designed to undermine the Indians' moneylending interests in the Turkestan Krai, Russian colonial Central Asia. Later in the nineteenth century, as opportunities in the region dwindled, Indians sought methods to transfer their wealth and relocate elsewhere. In the neighbouring Bukharan Amirate, Indian merchants were active in urban and rural markets for another several decades. A small number of Shikarpuris remained in the region even after the Bolshevik Revolution, but they did not last long under the Soviet Union.

As one would expect, historical circumstances unfolded quite differently in other markets. In Iran, notwithstanding the severe disruptions in the second quarter of the eighteenth century, Indian firms remained active from the sixteenth century even up to the modern day. To cite one exceptional example, in 1914, as opportunities in Central Asia were drawing to a close, a young Shikarpuri man named Parmanand Deepchand Hinduja (1901–71) moved from his native Shikarpur to Bombay. He established a new firm there, and five years later he moved his operational centre from India to Iran. At first, Parmanand Hinduja used his international connections to develop an import and export trade in Indian textiles, sugar and tea on the one hand, and Iranian fruit, carpets and saffron on the other. As his four sons grew into adulthood, the Hinduja family added profitable interests in dubbed Bollywood films.

Shortly after the family patriarch passed away in 1971, the Hinduja brothers used their close relationship with the Shah's government to navigate their way into a highly lucrative mediatory position between Iran and Indira Gandhi's government in India. The firm physically moved to Europe in the wake of the Islamic Revolution in 1979, but the Hinduja firm has earned distinction as one of only a very few of the Shah's business partners to enjoy a similarly close commercial relationship with the Islamic Republic—one that allegedly includes a questionable role in providing weapons to Iran through the international arms trade. Over the course of the twentieth century, the Hindujas' trade diversified to include ownership stakes in Gulf Oil International, Ashok Leyland commercial vehicles, Amas Bank in Switzerland, and a great variety of entertainment, software development, telecommunications, media and other interests. In just two generations, this modest Shikarpuri firm grew to become one of the wealthiest intercontinental business empires in the world today, with more than 70,000 employees working in 35 countries and assets worth an estimated $35 billion.

In Afghanistan, Indians maintained an active commercial presence right up to 1947. In the end, the socio-political trauma associated with partition dislocated the Indians' trade networks and precipitated the mass migration of the Multani-Shikarpuri firms from Pakistan, largely to Bombay. From there, Indian firms directed their attention away from Afghanistan and Central Asia in favour of emerging commercial opportunities that extend literally across the globe. As Markovits has demonstrated, by the beginning of the twenty-first century, large numbers of Multani-Shikarpuri merchants operated a vast network of communities that stretches from Hong Kong, Manila and Singapore in the East, across the Gulf, Africa and Europe, to the Caribbean islands, Central America, Canada and the United States in the west. Their ambitions, like their network, know no bounds.

NOTES

Introduction by Gurcharan Das

1. Quoted in Stephen Dale, *Indian Merchants and Eurasian Trade, 1600-1750*, Cambridge, UK: Cambridge University Press, 1944, p. 1.
2. Muzaffar Alam, 'Trade, State Policy and Regional Change: Aspects of Mughal-Uzbek Commercial Relations, C. 1550-1750', *Journal of the Economic and Social History of the Orient* 37, 3 (1994), p. 205, fn. 7.
3. Ibid., p. 221. I have quoted the verses with minor editing.
4. Ibid., p. 221.

1. Introduction

1. For a recent example, see Christopher I. Beckwith, *Empires of the Silk Road: A History of Central Eurasia*

from the Bronze Age to the Present, Princeton, 2009, pp. 232–62. I have critiqued the Orientalist methodology that underpins this interpretation in Scott C. Levi, 'Early Modern Central Asia in World History', *History Compass* 10, 11 (2012), pp. 866–78. For a more complete treatment of the historiography, see my earlier discussion, Scott Levi, 'India, Russia, and the Eighteenth-century Transformation of the Central Asian Caravan Trade', *Journal of the Social and Economic History of the Orient*, 42, 4 (1999), pp. 519–48, reprinted in Scott C. Levi, ed., *India and Central Asia: Commerce and Culture, 1500–1800*, New Delhi, 2007, pp. 93–122.

2. Merchants and the State

1. Wheeler M. Thackston, *The Baburnama: Memoirs of Babur, Prince and Emperor*, New York, 2002, p. 153.
2. 'Abbas Khan Sarwani, *Tarikh-i Sher Shah*, 2 vols, ed. by S.M. Imamuddin, Dacca, 1964, vol. 1, pp. 216–18; vol. 2, pp. 170–72.
3. Abul Fazl Allami, *The Ain-i Akbari*, 3 vols, tr. by H. Blochmann, 2d ed., Delhi, 1997, vol. 2, p. 405.
4. Abul Fazl Allami, *The Akbar Nama of Abu-l-Fazl*, 3 vols, tr. by Henry Beveridge, Delhi, 1998, vol. 3, pp. 520–21.

5. Eskandar Beg Monshi, *History of Shah 'Abbas the Great*, 2 vols, tr. by Roger M. Savory, Boulder, 1978, vol. 1, p. 523.

6. See the exceptionally detailed study by Audrey Burton, *The Bukharans: A Dynastic, Diplomatic and Commercial History, 1550–1702*, New York, 1997.

7. Mirakshah Munshi, Mullah Zahid Munshi and Muhammad Tahir Wahid, comps, *Maktubat Munsha'at Manshurat*, Abu Rayhan al-Beruni Oriental Studies Institute of the Academy of Sciences, Republic of Uzbekistan (OSIASRU), Ms. No. 289, fol. 67b.

8. Ibid., fol. 73a.

9. Ibid., fols 1b-2a.

10. Ibid., fol. 7a.

11. François Bernier, *Travels in the Mogul Empire, AD 1656–1668*, tr. by Irving Brock and ed. by Archibald Constable, Westminster, 1891, pp. 203–04, 249.

3. Multanis and Shikarpuris

1. Zia ud-Din Barani, *Tarikh-i-Firuz Shahi*, ed. by Saiyid Ahmad Khan, W.N. Lees and Kabiruddin, Bib. Ind., Calcutta, 1860–62, p. 120. The translation is found in Tapan Raychaudhuri and Irfan Habib, eds, *The Cambridge Economic*

History of India, 2 vols, Cambridge, 1982, vol. 1, p. 86.

2. Anthony Jenkinson, *Early Voyages and Travels to Russia and Persia . . .*, ed. by E. Delmar Morgan and C.H. Coote., Hakluyt Society Publications, 2 vols, 1st ser., nos 72–73, London, 1886, vol. 1, p. 87.

3. P.P. Ivanov, *Khoziaistvo dzhuibarskikh sheikhov: k istorii feodal'nogo zemlevladeniia v Srednei Azii v XVI– XVII vv.*, Moscow, 1954, doc. 49, pp. 122–23.

4. Hafiz Tanish, *Sharaf-Nama-i-Shahi*, OSIASRU Ms. No. 2207, fol. 451a–b.

5. *Majmu'a-i-Watha'iq*, OSIASRU Ms. No. 1386, fols 182a–b, 187b, 189a–b. For English-language translations, see appendix one of Levi, *The Indian Diaspora and Its Trade*, pp. 267–69.

6. John Chardin, *The Coronation of This Present King of Persia, Solyman the Third*, 1671, appended to *The Travels of Sir John Chardin into Persia and the East-Indies . . .*, London, 1686, p. 100.

7. Muhammad Yusuf Munshi, *Tadhkira-i Muqim Khani*, OSIASRU Ms. No. 609/II, fols 311b–14a.

8. Barani, *Tarikh-i Firuz Shahi*, pp. 120, 164, 310–12.

9. See the volume in this series by Muzaffar Alam and Sanjay Subrahmanyam.

10. Jean-Baptiste Tavernier, *Travels in India*, 2nd ed. 2 vols, ed. by William Crooke and tr. by V. Ball, 1676, reprint, New Delhi, 1995, vol. 1, p. 24.

11. See the volume in this series by Thomas A. Timberg, *The Marwaris: From Jagat Seth to the Birlas*, New Delhi, 2014.

12. Alexander Burnes, *Travels into Bukhara*, 3 vols, London, 1834, vol. 1, pp. 169–70.

13. B.R. Grover, 'An Integrated Pattern of Commercial Life in the Rural Society of North India during the Seventeenth and Eighteenth Centuries', in *Indian Historical Records Commission, Proceedings from the Thirty-Seventh Session*, Delhi, 1966, pp. 121–53.

14. Barani, *Tarikh-i Firzu Shahi*, pp. 298, 353.

15. Ivanov, *Khoziaistvo dzhuibarskikh sheikhov*, pp. 122–23.

16. *Majmu'a-i-watha'iq*, doc. 644, fol. 189b.

17. Ibid., fols 2a–b, 182b, 187b, 189a–b, 192a.

18. A.Sh. Shamansurova, 'Noviie danniie po istorii Afganistana (Orenburgskii Gosudarstvennii Arkhiv)', in M.G. Nikulin, ed., *Ocherki po novoi istorii Afganistana*, Tashkent, 1966, pp. 111–12.

19. Jean-Baptiste Tavernier, *Les six voyages de Jean-Baptiste Tavernier, Ecuyer Baron d'Aubonne . . .*, 2 vols, Utrecht, 1712, vol. 1, p. 62.

20. Jean de Thévenot, *The Travels of Monsieur de Thévenot, the Third Part, Containing the Relations of Indostan, the New Moguls, and of Other People and Countries of the Indies*, tr. Archibald Lovell, vol. 3, London, 1687, p. 55.

21. Muzaffar Alam, 'Trade, State Policy and Regional Change: Aspects of Mughal-Uzbek Commercial Relations, c.1550–1750', *Journal of the Economic and Social History of the Orient* 37, 3 (1994), p. 216.

22. Ibid., pp. 216–19.

23. Thévenot, *The Travels of Monsieur de Thévenot*, pp. 55–56.

24. Mountstuart Elphinstone, *An Account of the Kingdom of Caubul*, 3rd ed., 2 vols, London, 1839, vol. 1, pp. 413–14.

25. See R.V. Russell, *Tribes and Castes of the Central Provinces of India*, 4 vols, London, 1916, vol. 3, pp. 458–59.

26. L.C. Jain, *Indigenous Banking in India*, London, 1929, p. 32.

4. Indian Merchants in Central Asia

1. Jenkinson, *Early Voyages and Travels*, vol. 1, pp. 87–88 and notes 2–3.

2. Bernier, *Travels in the Mogul Empire, AD 1656–1668*, p. 202.

3. Raphaël du Mans, *Estat de la Perse in 1660*, Paris, 1890, p. 192.

4. *Maktubat*, fols 185b–186a.

5. Burnes, *Travels into Bukhara*, vol. 1, pp. 285–86.

6. Eugene Schuyler, *Turkistan: Notes of a Journey in Russian Turkistan, Khokand, Bukhara, and Kuldja*, 2 vols, New York, 1877, vol. 1, p. 186.

7. Mir Muhammad Amin Bukharai, *'Ubaydullahnama*, OSIASRU, Ms. No. 1532, fol. 203a–b. See also the Russian translation, A.A. Semenov, *Ubaidullah-name*, Tashkent, 1957, pp. 225–26.

8. Arminius Vámbéry, *Travels in Central Asia*, London, 1864, p. 372.

9. Charles Masson, *Narrative of Various Journeys in Balochistan, Afghanistan, the Panjab, & Kalat . . .*, 4 vols, London, 1844, vol. 1, p. 353.

10. Burnes, *Travels into Bukhara*, vol. 3, p. 111.

11. See Claude Markovits, *The Global World of Indian Merchants, 1750–1947: Traders of Sind from Bukhara to Panama*, Cambridge, 2000. See also his more recent state-of-the-field essay, 'Indian Merchants in Central Asia: The Debate', in Scott C. Levi, ed., *India and Central Asia: Commerce and Culture, 1500–1800*, Delhi, 2007, pp. 123–51.

12. Mohan Lal, *Travels in the Panjab, Afghanistan, Turkistan, to Balkh, Bokhara and Herat . . .*, London, 1846, p. 438.

13. Petros di Sarkis Gilanentz, *The Chronicle of Petros di Sarkis Gilanentz Concerning the Afghan Invasion of Persia in 1722, the Siege of Isfahan and the Repercussions in Northern Persia, Russia and Turkey*, tr. by Caro Minasian, Lisbon, 1959, pp. 35–36.

5. Indian Textiles

1. Niccolao Manucci, *Storia do Mogor, or Mogul India, 1653–1708*, 4 vols, London, 1907–8, vol. 2, p. 418.

2. John Bostock and H.T. Riley, trs., *The Natural History of Pliny*, 2 vols, London, 1855, vol. 2, p. 63.

3. Lionel Casson, tr., *The Periplus Maris Erythraei*, Princeton, 1989, p. 16.

4. K.N. Chaudhuri, 'The Structure of Indian Textile Industry in the Seventeenth and Eighteenth Centuries', *The Indian Economic and Social History Review* 11, 2–3 (1974), p. 127.

5. John Chardin, *Sir John Chardin's Travels in Persia*, London, 1927, pp. 278–79.

6. Alam, 'Trade, State Policy and Regional Change', p. 222.

7. *Majmu'a-i-Watha'iq*, fol. 229a.

8. William Foster, ed., 'Henry Bornford's Account of His Journey from Agra to Tatta', in *The English Factories in India 1637–1641*, Oxford, 1912, pp. 134–35.

9. I. Nizamutdinov, *Iz istorii Sredneaziatsko-indiiskikh otnoshenii, (IX–XVIII vv.)*, Tashkent, 1969, p. 50.

10. *Maktubat*, fols 5b–6a.

6. The Slave Trade

1. Abu Nasr Muhammad al-'Utbi, *Tarikh al-Yamini*, Delhi, 1847, pp. 395–408.

2. Muhammad Qasim Firishta, *Tarikh-i-Firishta*, Lucknow, 1864, pp. 27–28, 48–49.

3. Minhaj al-Siraj Juzjani, *Tabaqat-i Nasiri*, tr. by H.G. Raverty, 2 vols, New Delhi, 1970.

4. Ibid., vol. 1, pp. 522–23.

5. Barani, *Tarikh-i-Firuz Shahi*, pp. 45, 341.

6. Ibid., pp. 57–59.

7. Father Antonio Monserrate, *The Commentary of Father Monserrate, S. J., on His Journey to the Court of Akbar*, tr. by J.S. Hoyland, annot. by S.N. Banerjee, London, 1922, p. 117.

8. Francisco Pelsaert, *A Dutch Chronicle of Mughal India*, tr. and ed. by Brij Narain and Sri Ram Sharma, Lahore, 1978, p. 48.

9. Muhammad Yusuf Munshi bin Khwaja Baqa, *Tadhkira-i Muqim Khani*, OSIASRU, Ms. No. 609/ II, fols 323a–24a. Russian tr. by A.A. Semenov under the title *Mukimkhanskaia istoriia*, Tashkent, 1956.

10. *Majmu'a-i-Watha'iq*, fols 3a–50b.

11. Muhammad Talib, *Matlab al-Talibin*, OSIASRU, Ms. No. 80, fols 48a, 117a–18a, 198b.

12. Burnes, *Travels into Bukhara*, vol. 1, p. 276.

7. Horses

1. Ibn Battuta, *The Travels of Ibn Battuta, A.D. 1325– 1354*, tr. by H.A.R. Gibb, 3 vols, New Delhi, 1993, vol. 2, p. 478 and note 242.

2. Jos Gommans, *The Rise of the Indo-Afghan Empire, c.1710–1780*, Leiden, 1995.

3. Thévenot, *The Travels of Monsieur de Thévenot*, p. 44.

4. Marco Polo, *The Book of Ser Marco Polo*, 2 vols, ed. and tr. by Sir Henry Yule, New York, 1903, vol. 2, pp. 340, 348–49.

5. Afanasi (Athanasius) Nikitin, *The Travels of Athanasius Nikitin of Twer*, in R.H. Major, ed., *India in the Fifteenth Century*, London, 1857, part 3, p. 19.

6. Thackston, *The Baburnama*, p. 153.

7. Bernier, *Travels in the Mogul Empire*, p. 203.

8. Tavernier, *Les six voyages*, vol. 2, p. 63.

9. Thévenot, *The Travels of Monsieur de Thévenot*, p. 57.

10. Manucci, *Storia do Mogor*, vol. 2, pp. 390–91.

11. Comte de Modave, *Voyage en Inde du Comte de Modave, 1773–1776*, ed. by J. Deloche, Paris, 1971, p. 327.

12. Gommans, *The Rise of the Indo-Afghan Empire*, p. 89.

8. The Life and Death of a Diaspora

1. Josiah Harlan, *Central Asia: Personal Narrative of General Josiah Harlan, 1823–1841*, ed. by Frank E. Ross, London, 1939, p. 65.

2. Thomas Herbert, *Some Years Travels into Divers Parts of Africa, and Asia the Great. . .*, London, 1638, p. 78.

3. Thévenot, *The Travels of Monsieur de Thévenot*, pp. 57–58.

4. Burnes, *Travels to Bukhara*, vol. 1, p. 169.

5. George Forster, *A Journey from Bengal to England*, 2 vols, London, 1798, vol. 2, p. 151.

6. 'Abstract of Captain Christie's Journal', in Henry Pottinger, *Travels in Beloochistan and Sinde . . .*, London, 1816, p. 415.

7. J.P. Ferrier, *Caravan Journeys and Wanderings in Persia, Afghanistan, Turkistan, and Beloochistan . . .*, ed. by

H.D. Seymour and tr. by Capt. William Jesse, London, 1856, p. 454.

8. W. Moorcroft and G. Trebek, *Travels in the Himalayan Provinces of Hindustan and the Panjab; in Ladak and Kashmir, in Peshawar, Kabul, Kunduz, and Bokhara; by Mr. William Moorcroft and Mr. George Trebeck, from 1819 to 1825*, 2 vols, London, 1841, vol. 2, pp. 413, 437.

9. Fayz Muhammad Katib, *Siraj al-tawarikh*, 3 vols, Kabul, 1913–15, vol. 3, p. 921.

10. Elphinstone, *An Account of the Kingdom of Caubul*, vol. 1, pp. 333–34.

11. Henry Pottinger, *Travels in Beloochistan and Sinde . . .*, London, 1816, passim.

12. *Maktubat*, fols 185b–86a.

13. Mohan Lal, *Travels in the Panjab*, p. 137.

14. G.L. Dmitriev, 'Iz istorii Indiiskikh kolonii v Srednei Azii (vtoraia polovina XIX–nachalo XX v.)', in D.A. Ol'derogge, ed., *Strani i narodi vostoka*, vol. 12, part 2, *Indiia: strana i narod*. Moscow, 1972, p. 88.

15. Sadr al-Din 'Aini, *Yoddoshtho*, 4 vols, Stalinabad (Dushanbe), 1949–54, vol. 3, pp. 77–78.

16. Vámbéry, *Travels in Central Asia*, p. 372.

17. Ibid.

18. Ole Olufsen, *The Emir of Bokhara and His Country: Journeys and Studies in Bokhara*, London, 1911, pp. 296–97.

19. Chardin, *Sir John Chardin's Travels in Persia*, pp. 280–81.

20. Jenkinson, *Early Voyages and Travels*, vol. 1, p. 149.

21. Ibid., vol. 2, appendix IX, pp. 428–29.

22. Pietro Della Valle, *I Viaggi Di Pietro Della Valle: Lettere Dalla Persia*, ed. by F. Gaeta and L. Lockhart, Rome, 1972, p. 39.

23. Adam Olearius, *The Voyages and Travels of the Ambassadors Sent by Frederick Duke of Holstein, to the Great Duke of Muscovy, and the King of Persia . . .*, tr. by John Davies, London, 1667, p. 299.

24. John Fryer, *A New Account of East India and Persia, Being Nine Years' Travels, 1672–1681*, 3 vols, ed. with notes by William Crooke, London, 1912–15, vol. 2, p. 216.

25. John Chardin, *The Travels of Sir John Chardin into Persia and the East-Indes . . . to Which Is Added, the Coronation of this Present King of Persia, Solyman the Third*, London, 1686, p. 100.

26. Niels Steensgaard, *The Asian Trade Revolution of the Seventeenth Century: the East India Companies and the Decline of the Caravan Trade*, Chicago, 1974, p. 410.

27. Edward Scott Waring, *A Tour to Sheeraz*, London, 1807, pp. 3–4.

28. George Keppel, *Personal Narrative of a Journey from India to England . . . in the Year 1824*, London, 1827, p. 294.

29. George Curzon, *Persia and the Persian Question*, 2 vols, London, 1892, vol. 1, p. 291.

30. K.A. Antonova and N.M. Gol'dberg, eds, *Russko-indiiskie otnosheniia v XVIII v., sbornik dokumentov*, Moscow, 1965 (Antonova II); K.A. Antonova, N.M. Gol'dberg and T.D. Lavrentsova, eds, *Russko-indiiskie otnosheniia v XVII v., sbornik dokumentov*, Moscow, 1958 (Antonova I); Surendra Gopal, *Indians in Russia in the 17th and 18th Centuries*, Calcutta, 1988.

31. Antonova II, doc. 37, 1723, pp. 57–59.

32. Peter Henry Bruce, *Memoirs of Peter Henry Bruce . . .* Dublin, 1783, p. 299.

33. Surendra Gopal, 'Trading Activities of Indians in Russia in the Eighteenth Century', *The Indian Economic and Social History Review* 5, 2 (1968), p. 142. Gopal's information comes from Antonova II, doc. 114, 1745, pp. 211–34.

34. Antonova II, doc. 69, 1735, pp. 128–33.

35. Comte de Modave, *Voyage en Inde*, p. 405. Although identified as Gujarati, one wonders whether they were actually Powindas undertaking their annual migration northwards.

36. Mir Izzet Ullah, 'Travels beyond the Himalaya, by Mir Izzet Ullah. Republished from the Calcutta Oriental Quarterly Magazine, 1825', *Journal of the Royal Asiatic Society* VII (1843), p. 332.

37. The culmination of their efforts is documented in an archival folder titled 'O paralizaovanii ekspluatsii tuzemnogo nasaleniia indeiskimi vykhodtsami' ('Regarding the Paralization of the Exploitation of the Native Population by Indian Immigrants'), Central State Historical Archive of the Republic of Uzbekistan, fond I–1, opis' 11, delo 39 , 25 June 1877—10 April 1893.

38. Ibid., lists 16–17ob.

39. Ibid., list 27–27ob.

40. F.M. Bailey, *Mission to Tashkent*, London, 1946, p. 30.

41. Markovits, *The Global World of Indian Merchants*, p. 105.

BIBLIOGRAPHY

Selected Primary Sources

'Abbas Khan Sarwani. *Tarikh-i Sher Shahi*. 2 vols. Edited by S.M. Imamuddin. Dacca, 1964.

Abul Fazl Allami. *The Ain-i Akbari*. 3 vols. Translated by Henry Blochman. 1927. Reprint. Delhi, 1997.

——. *The Akbar Nama of Abu-l Fazl*. 3 vols. Translated by Henry Beveridge. 1902–39. Reprint. Delhi, 1998.

'Aini, Sadr al-Din. *Dokhunda*. Kazan, 1931.

——. *Yoddoshtho*. Vols 3 and 4. Stalinabad (Dushanbe), 1949–54.

Antonova, K.A., and N.M. Gol'dberg, eds. *Russko-indiiskie otnosheniia v XVIII v., sbornik dokumentov*. Moscow, 1965 (Antonova II).

Antonova, K.A., N.M. Gol'dberg and T.D. Lavrentsova, eds. *Russko-indiiskie otnosheniia v XVII v., sbornik dokumentov*. Moscow, 1958 (Antonova I).

Bailey, F.M. *Mission to Tashkent*. London, 1946.

Bernier, François. *Travels in the Mogul Empire, AD 1656–1668*. Translated by Irving Brock and edited by Archibald Constable. Westminster, 1891.

Bruce, Peter Henry. *Memoirs of Peter Henry Bruce* . . . Dublin, 1783.

Burnes, Alexander. *Cabool: A Personal Narrative of a Journey to, and Residence in that City, in the Years 1836, 7, and 8* . . . 2d edition. London, 1843.

——. *Travels into Bokhara* . . . 3 vols. London, 1834.

Chardin, John. *Sir John Chardin's Travels in Persia*. London, 1927.

——. *The Travels of Sir John Chardin into Persia and the East-Indies . . . to Which Is Added, the Coronation of This Present King of Persia, Solyman the Third*. London, 1686.

——. *Voyages du Chevalier Chardin, en Perse, et Autres Lieux de l'Orient*. 10 vols. Paris, 1811.

Della Valle, Pietro. *I Viaggi Di Pietro Della Valle: Lettere Dalla Persia*. Edited by F. Gaeta and L. Lockhart. Rome, 1972.

——. *The Pilgrim, the Travels of Pietro della Valle*. Edited and translated by George Bull. London, 1989.

Elphinstone, Mountstuart. *An Account of the Kingdom of Caubul, and Its Dependencies, in Persia, Tartary, and India* . . . 3d edition. 2 vols. London, 1839.

Eskandar Beg Monshi. *History of Shah 'Abbas the Great: Tarik-e 'Alamara-ye 'Abbasi*. 2 vols. Translated by Roger M. Savory. Boulder, 1978.

Fayz Muhammad Katib. *Siraj al-tawarikh*. 3 vols. Kabul, 1913–15.

Ferrier, J.P. *Caravan Journeys and Wanderings in Persia, Afghanistan, Turkistan, and Beloochistan* . . . Edited by H.D. Seymour and translated by Capt. William Jesse. London, 1856.

Forster, George. *A Journey from Bengal to England*. 2 vols. 1798. Reprint. Delhi, 1970.

Fryer, John. *A New Account of East India and Persia, Being Nine Years' Travels, 1672–1681*. 3 vols. Edited, with notes, by William Crooke. Hakluyt Society Publications, 2d ser., nos 19–20, 39. London, 1912–15.

Gilanentz, Petros di Sarkis. *The Chronicle of Petros di Sarkis Gilanentz Concerning the Afghan Invasion of Persia in 1722, the Siege of Isfahan and the Repercussions in Northern Persia, Russia and Turkey*. Translated by Caro Owen Minasian. Lisbon, 1959.

Gopal, Surendra. *Indians in Russia in the 17th and 18th Centuries*. Calcutta, 1988.

Hafiz Tanish. *Sharaf-nama-i-shahi*. Abu Rayhan al-Beruni Oriental Studies Institute of the Academy of Sciences of the Republic of Uzbekistan (OSIASRU), Manuscript No. 2207.

Harlan, Josiah. *Central Asia: Personal Narrative of General Josiah Harlan, 1823–1841*. Edited by Frank E. Ross. London, 1939.

Herbert, Thomas. *Some Years Travels into Divers Parts of Africa, and Asia the Great...*, London, 1638.

Ibn Battuta, *The Travels of Ibn Battuta, A.D. 1325–1354*. Translated by H.A.R. Gibb. 3 vols. Reprint. New Delhi, 1993.

Ivanov, P.P. *Khoziaistvo dzhuibarskikh sheikhov: k istorii feodal'nogo zemlevladeniia v Srednei Azii v XVI–XVII vv*. Moscow, 1954.

Mir Izzet Ullah, 'Travels beyond the Himalaya, by Mir Izzet Ullah. Republished from the Calcutta Oriental Quarterly Magazine, 1825'. *Journal of the Royal Asiatic Society* VII (1843), pp. 283–342.

Mir Muhammad Amin Bukharai, *'Ubaydullahnama*, OSIASRU, Manuscript No. 1532.

Jenkinson, Anthony. *Early Voyages and Travels to Russia and Persia* . . . Edited by E. Delmar Morgan and

C.H. Coote. Hakluyt Society Publications. 2 vols. 1st ser., nos 72–73. London, 1886.

Kaempfer, Engelbert. *Am Hofe des persischen Grosskönigs 1684–1685*. Edited by Walter Hinz. Tübingen, Basel, 1977.

Keppel, George. *Personal Narrative of a Journey from India to England . . . in the Year 1824*. London, 1827.

Lal, Mohan. *Travels in the Panjab, Afghanistan, Turkistan, to Balkh, Bokhara and Herat . . .* London, 1846.

Majmu'a-i-watha'iq. OSIASRU, Manuscript No. 1386.

du Mans, Raphaël. *Estat de la Perse en 1660*. Paris, 1890.

Manucci, Niccolao. *Storia do Mogor, or Mogul India 1653– 1708*. 4 vols. Translated by W. Irvine. London, 1907–08.

Masson, Charles. *Narrative of Various Journeys in Balochistan, Afghanistan, the Panjab, & Kalât . . .* 4 vols. London, 1844.

Meyendorff, E.K. *Puteshestvie iz Orenburga v Bukharu*. Translated from the Russian by N.A. Khalfin. Moscow, 1975.

de Modave, Comte. *Voyage en Inde du Comte de Modave, 1773–1776*. Edited by J. Deloche. Paris, 1971.

Moorcroft, W. and G. Trebek. *Travels in the Himalayan Provinces of Hindustan and the Panjab; in Ladak and Kashmir, in Peshawar, Kabul, Kunduz, and Bokhara; by Mr. William Moorcroft and Mr. George Trebeck, from 1819 to 1825*. 2 vols. London, 1841.

Muhammad Yusuf Munshi. *Tadhkira-i Muqim Khani*. OSIASRU, Manuscript No. 609/II.

Olearius Adam. *The Voyages and Travels of the Ambassadors Sent by Frederick Duke of Holstein, to the Great Duke of Muscovy, and the King of Persia . . .* Translated by John Davies. London, 1667.

Olufsen, Ole. *The Emir of Bokhara and His Country: Journeys and Studies in Bokhara*. London, 1911.

Pallas, Peter Simon. *Travels through the Southern Provinces of the Russian Empire, in the Years 1793 and 1794*. 2 vols. Translated by Francis L. Bludgon. London, 1802–03.

Pottinger, Henry. *Travels in Beloochistan and Sinde . . .* London, 1816.

Schuyler, Eugene. *Turkistan: Notes of a Journey in Russian Turkistan, Khokand, Bukhara, and Kuldja.* 2 vols. New York, 1877.

Struys, John. *The Voyages and Travels of John Struys through Italy, Greece, Muscovy, Tartary, Media, Persia, East-India, Japan, and Other Countries in Europe, Africa and Asia . . .* Translated by John Morrison. London, 1684.

Tavernier, Jean-Baptiste. *Les six voyages de Jean-Baptiste Tavernier, Ecuyer Baron d'Aubonne.* 2 vols. Utrecht, 1712.

———. *Travels in India.* 2nd edition. 2 vols. Edited by William Crooke and translated by V. Ball. 1676. Reprint. New Delhi, 1995.

———. *Travels en Perse et description de ce royaume.* Paris, 1930.

Thackston, Wheeler M. *The Baburnama: Memoirs of Babur, Prince and Emperor.* New York, 2002.

de Thévenot, Jean. *The Travels of Monsieur de Thévenot, the Third Part, Containing the Relations of Indostan, the New Moguls, and of Other People and Countries of the Indies*. Translated by Archibald Lovell. Vol. 3. London, 1687.

Vámbéry, Arminius. *Travels in Central Asia*. London, 1864. Reprint edition, New York, 1970.

Waring, Edward Scott. *A Tour to Sheeraz* . . . London, 1807.

Zia ud-Din Barani. *Tarikh-i-Firuz Shahi*. Edited by Saiyid Ahmad Khan, W.N. Lees and Kabiruddin. Calcutta, 1860–62.

Selected Secondary Readings

Alam, Muzaffar. 'Trade, State Policy and Regional Change: Aspects of Mughal-Uzbek Commercial Relations, c.1550–1750'. *Journal of the Economic and Social History of the Orient* 37, 3 (1994), pp. 202–27.

Baikova, N.B. *Rol' Srednei Azii v russko-indiiskikh torgovikh sviaziakh*. Tashkent, 1964.

Banerji, Anup. *Old Routes: North Indian Nomads and Bankers in Afghan, Uzbek and Russian Lands*. Gurgaon, 2011.

Bhargava, Brijkishore. *Indigenous Banking in Ancient & Medieval India*. Bombay, 1934.

Burton, Audrey. *The Bukharans: a Dynastic, Diplomatic and Commercial History, 1550–1702*. New York, 1997.

Chaudhuri, K.N. *Trade and Civilisation in the Indian Ocean: An Economic History from the Rise of Islam to 1750*. Cambridge, 1985.

Chawla, Joginder K. *India's Overland Trade with Central Asia and Persia During the Thirteenth and Fourteenth Centuries*. New Delhi, 2006.

Dale, Stephen. *Indian Merchants and Eurasian Trade, 1600–1750*. Cambridge, 1994.

Deloche, Jean. *Transport and Communication in India Prior to Steam Locomotion*. Vol. 1. *Land Transport*. Translated by James Walker. Oxford University Press, 1993.

Dmitriev, G.L. 'Iz istorii Indiiskikh kolonii v Srednei Azii (vtoraia polovina XIX–nachalo XX v.)', in D.A. Ol'derogge, editor, *Strani i narodi vostoka*, vol. 12, part 2, *Indiia: strana i narod*. Moscow, 1972, pp. 234–47.

Gankovsky, Yu. 'The Durrani Empire'. In *Afghanistan Past and Present*. Translated by Evgeni Khazanov. Moscow, 1981, pp. 76–98.

Gommans, Jos. *The Rise of the Indo-Afghan Empire, c.1710–1780*. Leiden, 1995.

Gopal, Surendra. 'A Brief Note on Business Organisation of Indian Merchants in Russia in the 17th Century'. *Journal of the Economic and Social History of the Orient* 29, 1 (1986), pp. 205–12.

——. 'Indians in Central Asia, Sixteenth and Seventeenth Centuries'. Presidential Address, Medieval India Section of the Indian History Congress, New Delhi, February 1992. Patna, 1992.

Grover, B.R. 'An Integrated Pattern of Commercial Life in the Rural Society of North India during the Seventeenth and Eighteenth Centuries', in *Indian Historical Records Commission, Proceedings from the Thirty-Seventh Session*. Delhi, 1966, pp. 121–53.

Hanifi, Shah. *Connecting Histories in Afghanistan: Market Relations and State Formation on a Colonial Frontier*. Stanford, 2011.

Keyvani, Mehdi. *Artisans and Guild Life in the Later Safavid Period: Contributions to the Social-Economic History of Persia*. Berlin, 1982.

Jain, L.C. *Indigenous Banking in India*. London, 1929.

Levi, Scott C. 'Commercial Structures', in D. Morgan and A. Reid, eds, *The New Cambridge History of Islam*, vol. 3, *The Eastern Islamic World, 11th–18th Centuries*. Cambridge, 2012, pp. 561–81.

——. 'Early Modern Central Asia in World History'. *History Compass* 10, 11 (2012), pp. 866–78.

——. *The Indian Diaspora in Central Asia and Its Trade, 1550–1900*. Leiden, 2002.

——. 'Objects in Motion', in Douglas Northrop, ed., *A Companion to World History*. Oxford, 2012, pp. 321–38.

Levi, Scott C., ed. *India and Central Asia: Commerce and Culture, 1500–1800*. New Delhi, 2007.

Liu, Xinru, ed. *India and Central Asia*. Ranikhet, 2012.

Liusternik, E.Ia. *Russko-indiiskie ekonomicheskie nauchnie i kul'turnie sviazi v XIX v.* Moscow, 1966.

——. *Russko-indiiskie ekonomicheskie sviazi v XIX v.* Moscow, 1958.

Markovits, Claude. *The Global World of Indian Merchants, 1750–1947: Traders of Sind from Bukhara to Panama.* Cambridge, 2000.

——. *Merchants, Traders, Entrepreneurs: Indian Business in the Colonial Era.* New Delhi, 2008.

Matthee, Rudolph. *The Politics of Trade in Safavid Iran: Silk for Silver, 1600–1730.* Cambridge, 1999.

McChesney, R.D. *Central Asia: Foundations of Change.* Princeton, 1996.

Mukminova, R.G. *Sotsial'naia differentsiatsiia naseleniia gorodov Uzbekistana v XV–XVI vv.* Tashkent, 1985.

Nizamutdinov, Il'ias. *Iz istorii Sredneaziatsko-indiiskikh otnoshenii, (IX–XVIII vv.).* Tashkent, 1969.

Nizomiddinov, I.Gh. *XVI–XVIII asrlarda Orta Osiyo–Hindiston munosabatlari*. Tashkent, 1966.

Rasul'-Zade, P.N. *Iz istorii Sredneaziatsko-indiiskikh sviazei vtoroi poloviny XIX–nachala XX veka*. Tashkent, 1968.

Shkunov, V.N. 'Russko-indiiskaia torgovlia na Sredneaziatskikh rinkakh v kontse XVIII–nachale XIX v. (po materialam Rossiyskikh arkhivov)'. *Vostok, Afro-aziatskie obshchestva: istoriya i sovremennost'* 3 (1997), pp. 94–101.

Steensgaard, Niels. *The Asian Trade Revolution of the Seventeenth Century: The East India Companies and the Decline of the Caravan Trade*. Chicago, 1974.

Subrahmanyam, Sanjay and C.A. Bayly. 'Portfolio Capitalists and the Political Economy of Early Modern India'. *The Indian Economic and Social History Review* 25, 4 (1988), pp. 401–24.

Tripathi, Dwijendra, ed. *Business Communities of India: A Historical Perspective*. New Delhi, 1984.